La visión Psicoanalítica de
CARL GUSTAV JUNG
Un camino terapéutico hacia la transformación

Sinuhe Ulises García Reynoso

Reservados todos los derechos. No se permite la reproducción total o parcial de esta obra, ni su incorporación a un sistema informático, ni su transmisión en cualquier forma o por cualquier medio (electrónico, mecánico, fotocopia, grabación u otros) sin autorización previa y por escrito de los titulares del copyright, excepto breves citas y con la fuente identificada correctamente.. La infracción de dichos derechos puede constituir un delito contra la propiedad intelectual.

El contenido de esta obra es responsabilidad del autor y no refleja necesariamente las opiniones de la casa editora. Todos los textos e imágenes fueron proporcionados por el autor, quien es el único responsable por los derechos de los mismos.

Publicado por Ibukku, LLC
www.ibukku.com
Diseño de portada: Ángel Flores Guerra Bistrain
Diseño y maquetación: Diana Patricia González Juárez
Copyright © 2024 Sinhue Ulises García Reynoso
ISBN Paperback: 978-1-68574-816-6
ISBN Hardcover: 978-1-68574-818-0
ISBN eBook: 978-1-68574-817-3

Dedication

This book is dedicated to all the young adults and new adults navigating the exhilarating and often turbulent waters of early adulthood. To those who find themselves juggling career aspirations, financial anxieties, and the complexities of love and relationships, may this story offer a comforting reminder that you are not alone. It's dedicated to those who dare to dream big, even when the path ahead seems daunting, and who find the strength to overcome obstacles, whether it's navigating challenging relationships, managing unexpected pregnancies, or simply figuring out how to pay rent while simultaneously chasing your passions. This story is for you – a testament to the resilience of the human spirit, the power of love in its many forms, and the unwavering belief in a brighter future. It's a celebration of the messy, beautiful, and often chaotic journey of growing up and finding your place in the world, with all its triumphs and heartbreaks. May it serve as a source of both entertainment and inspiration, a comforting companion during moments of uncertainty, and a gentle reminder that even in the midst of chaos, love can endure, grow, and ultimately, prevail. This is a tribute to your strength, your courage, and your unwavering spirit.

Preface

Writing this story has been a journey of its own. The characters of Keith and Sira, their love, their struggles, their triumphs – they've become companions, reflections of the many young adults I've encountered, both in my own life and through the stories I've heard. This book delves into the realities of young adulthood: the financial pressures that can strain even the strongest relationships, the anxieties that accompany unexpected pregnancies, the complexities of navigating past relationships and maintaining healthy friendships. It's not a fairy tale; it's a glimpse into the messy, beautiful, and sometimes heartbreaking reality of growing up and building a life together. I hope this story resonates with readers, offering both entertainment and a sense of connection. It is my hope that this portrayal of Keith and Sira's journey will both entertain and inspire. That it will spark discussions on important topics such as communication in relationships, financial pressures, and the challenges of early parenthood. I've tried to capture the nuances of their emotions, their vulnerabilities, and their resilience. I've aimed to create characters that are both flawed and relatable, imperfect yet deeply human. Their story is one of overcoming challenges, navigating complexities, and ultimately, finding strength and growth in the face of adversity. I've drawn inspiration from countless conversations, observations, and personal experiences to paint a vivid and honest portrayal of young adulthood. While this story is fictional, its themes are profoundly real, and I hope it will leave readers feeling seen, understood, and inspired.

Introduction

This story begins with an unexpected pregnancy, a life-altering event that throws Keith and Sira's college romance into a whirlwind of unforeseen challenges. While the joy of a new life is undeniable, it's quickly intertwined with the anxieties of financial instability, the pressures of starting a family prematurely, and the complex web of relationships that surround them. Keith's lingering connections with his ex-girlfriends create a source of tension and insecurity for Sira, a young woman already grappling with the significant changes in her life. As their relationship navigates this stormy sea, their communication breaks down, misunderstandings breed resentment, and their future together hangs precariously in the balance. To add another layer of complexity, Sira's high school ex-boyfriend re-emerges, introducing unforeseen dilemmas. This introduction sets the stage for a journey of self-discovery, resilience, and the strength found in love and commitment. We will follow Sira and Keith as they grapple with the overwhelming realities of adult life, revealing the emotional roller coaster of their journey. It's a story about facing vulnerabilities, overcoming obstacles, and the ultimate strength found in facing life's uncertainties together. It's about the messy realities of love, the importance of open communication, and the profound impact that unexpected events can have on young lives. This story is about the journey itself, not just the destination; it's a exploration of the complex dynamics of relationships, the anxieties of early adulthood, and the resilience of the human spirit. It's a testament to the power of love, the enduring strength of commitment, and the possibility of finding happiness even in the face of adversity.

Contents

Copyright 1
Dedication 2
Preface 4
Introduction 6
Chapter 1: 12
    The Pregnancy Announcement 12
    Doubts and Insecurities 19
    Fears and Anxieties 26
    Financial Strain and the House Purchase 34
    Who are They 41
Chapter 2: 50
    Therapy Sessions 50
    The Farther we Grow 58
    Reconciliation 65
    There She Is 72
    Growing Isolation 82
Chapter 3: 91
    The Heat 91
    An Apology with Understanding 99

Forgiveness and Acceptance 107

Addressing Financial Concerns 115

Strengthening Communication 123

Chapter 4: 131

Ex, High School 131

Emotional Storm 142

Reaction and Jealousy 151

A Confrontation with the Ex 162

Navigating the New Dynamic 172

Chapter 5 181

Repairing Broken Trust 181

Open Communication and Vulnerability 190

Understanding Past Relationships 198

Addressing Keiths Jealousy 208

Sira's Self-Discovery 216

Chapter 6 224

Prenatal Care and Challenges 224

Planning for the Baby's Arrival 231

Adjusting to New Roles 240

Support System and Family 248

Growing Closer Through Shared Experience 257

Chapter 7: 266

Labor and Delivery 266

    Welcoming the Baby 274

    The First Few Days 282

    Adjusting to Parenthood....................................... 291

    Shifting Dynamics 300

Chapter 8: 309

    Sleep Deprivation and Stress 309

    Relationship Strain... 317

    Seeking Support 327

    Redefining Roles 337

    The Balancing Act.. 347

Chapter 9: 357

    Overcoming Obstacles.. 357

    Strengthening Bonds 365

    Emotional Maturity 373

    Shared Dreams and Goals 381

    Celebrating Milestones 390

Chapter 10: 398

    Reflecting on the Journey.................................... 398

    Embracing the Future 406

    New Challenges and Opportunities 415

    A Stronger Foundation... 424

    The Lasting Impact of Love................................. 432

Acknowledgments 443

Author Biography 445

Chapter 1:

The Pregnancy Announcement

The air hung heavy with unspoken anxieties, thick with the scent of brewing coffee and the nervous energy thrumming between Sira and Keith. Sunlight streamed through the kitchen window, illuminating dust motes dancing in the golden rays, a stark contrast to the storm brewing inside Sira. She clutched the small, ultrasound photo in her hand, the grainy image, a tangible representation of the seismic shift about to occur in their lives. It felt surreal, this tiny life nestled within her, a secret she'd carried for weeks, a secret that threatened to unravel everything they'd painstakingly built.

She'd chosen this moment, this quiet Saturday morning, hoping for a gentle unveiling, a shared moment of joy. But the silence stretched, thick and suffocating, broken only by the rhythmic drip of the coffee maker. Keith, oblivious to the turmoil swirling within her, was engrossed in his phone, scrolling through some sports news, his brow furrowed in concentration. The casual indifference felt like a physical blow, a stark reminder of the chasm that had already begun to form between them.

Finally, Sira cleared her throat, the sound, brittle and strained. "Keith," she began, her voice barely a whisper, "there's something I need to tell you."

He looked up, his eyes meeting hers, and for a fleeting moment, Sira saw a flicker of genuine concern. Then, the concern morphed into something else – suspicion. A guardedness that chilled her to the bone.

"What is it, Sira?" he asked, his tone cautious, guarded.

She swallowed, the lump in her throat threatening to choke her. She placed the ultrasound photo on the table between them, its grainy image staring back at them, a silent witness to the impending drama. "I'm pregnant," she said, the words escaping in a rush, a confession rather than a joyous announcement.

The silence that followed was deafening. Keith stared at the photo, his expression unreadable. Sira braced herself, waiting for the outpouring of joy she'd envisioned, the shared elation of this miraculous news. But the joy didn't come. Instead, a wave of icy apprehension washed over her.

Keith picked up the photo, his fingers tracing the outline of the tiny fetus. He didn't speak, didn't react, his silence more damning than any outright rejection. Sira's heart sank. This wasn't the reaction she'd hoped for. This wasn't the romantic, movie-like scene she'd played out countless times in her head.

Finally, he looked up, his gaze sharp and questioning. "Are you sure?" he asked, his voice devoid of emotion. The question hung in the air, heavy with unspoken doubt. It wasn't a doubt about the pregnancy itself, but a doubt about her motives. A doubt that cut deeper than any accusation.

"Of course, I'm sure," Sira replied, her voice trembling slightly. "I have the test results, the ultrasound…"

"I'm just… surprised," he mumbled, avoiding her gaze. His words were unconvincing, a flimsy veil over a deeper unease. Sira knew instantly what he was thinking. He suspected this was some kind of elaborate ploy, a calculated move to manipulate him, to drive a wedge between him and his friends, his ex-girlfriends. The thought stung, a bitter pill to swallow.

He'd been so defensive lately, so quick to perceive betrayal where none existed. His ex-girlfriends, still present in his life, had cast a long shadow over their relationship, creating a constant undercurrent of insecurity and suspicion. Sira understood his anxieties, to an extent. She'd seen him struggle with the weight of his past relationships, the lingering feelings and attachments. But this? This was different. This was a life, a child, a future they were about to build together, or perhaps tear apart.

"Is this… about them?" she asked, her voice barely audible, the question hanging in the air like a poisoned dart.

He flinched, his eyes widening slightly. He knew exactly what she meant. The "them" were his exes, the women who still occupied a significant space in his life, the women who had, in Sira's eyes, created a toxic cloud of insecurity over their relationship. He knew the accusation was implied, not explicit, but the pain was palpable.

"No," he said, his voice strained, "it's not about them. I'm just… processing this. It's a lot."

His words were a hollow attempt at reassurance, a desperate plea to diminish the suspicion forming in Sira's eyes. But his unconvincing denials only intensified her fears. She knew him well enough to recognize the subtle shift in his demeanor, the careful avoidance of eye contact, the stiffening of his shoulders. He was building walls, erecting barriers between them, just as he'd done in the past.

The joy she'd felt just moments ago, the excitement of carrying a new life within her, was now overshadowed by a crushing wave of anxiety and uncertainty. The weight of this pregnancy, the weight of their precarious relationship, felt overwhelming. She'd imagined this moment countless times, imagined shared tears of joy, a future painted with vibrant colors. Instead, she was confronted with suspicion, doubt, and a chilling uncertainty about their future. The room felt cold, the sunlight no longer warm and inviting, but rather a harsh spotlight revealing the cracks in their foundation. This wasn't the beginning she'd hoped for. This was a battleground. And the war had just begun.

The silence stretched on, a painful testament to the unspoken accusations and unresolved anxieties hanging between them. Sira's mind raced, her thoughts a chaotic jumble of fear and hope, joy and despair. She was pregnant, yes, but was she also pregnant with the weight of their potential failure? Was this child destined to grow up in an atmosphere of mistrust and uncertainty?

The ultrasound photo lay between them, a silent testament to the fragility of their relationship and the monumental task that lay ahead. The future stretched before them, an uncharted territory filled with both promise and peril. The weight of it all pressed down on her, a suffocating blanket of anxiety. She had a lot to process, much more than Keith seemed to realize or acknowledge. The coffee, still brewing, seemed to mock their strained silence with its insistent dripping. The dust motes danced on, oblivious to the storm brewing between them, a storm that could either destroy or strengthen their precarious bond. The coming months, she knew, would be a test. A test of their love, their resilience, their very survival as a couple. And Sira, clutching the fragile hope of their future, was terrified of the outcome.

Doubts and Insecurities

The silence stretched, a taut, elastic band threatening to snap. Keith finally broke it, the sound of his voice rough, unfamiliar even to his own ears. "So," he began, the word hanging in the air like a question mark. He picked up the ultrasound photo, his fingers clumsy, hesitant. The grainy image seemed to mock him, a tiny, silent judge of his inadequacy. He hadn't even realized how much he'd been avoiding looking at it, preferring the blurry reality of his own denial to the stark truth staring back at him from the paper.

He looked up at Sira, her face a mask of quiet apprehension. The usual vibrant sparkle in her eyes was dimmed, replaced by a weary sadness that pierced him. He hadn't seen her this vulnerable before, this fragile. It hit him with the force of a physical blow, a sudden, sickening realization of how much he'd taken her for granted. He'd been so focused on his own anxieties, his own insecurities, that he'd failed to see the weight she carried.

His mind raced, a whirlwind of conflicting thoughts and emotions. He'd always prided himself on his ability to navigate relationships, on his maturity and understanding. He'd been the steady one, the reliable one, the one who always knew what to say and how to make things right. But now, faced with this monumental shift in their lives, he felt utterly lost.

The memory of his past relationships flickered through his mind, each a ghostly reminder of his own flaws. There was Chloe, the fiery artist who'd accused him of being emotionally unavailable. He'd dismissed her accusations then, chalking them up to her own insecurities. But now, looking at Sira's quiet desperation, he saw the chilling echo of Chloe's words in her eyes. Had he been emotionally unavailable all along? Had he simply buried his own vulnerabilities under a veneer of calm confidence?

Then there was Emily, the driven lawyer who'd left him because he wasn't ambitious enough. He'd felt stung by her rejection, believing she'd misunderstood him. He'd always prioritized stability and security, while she craved excitement and risk. Now, facing the uncertainty of fatherhood, he wondered if Emily had been right all along. Was he truly capable of providing the kind of life he wanted for Sira and their child?

The thought of providing, of being the solid rock Sira needed, filled him with a profound sense of inadequacy. He'd always been good at providing for himself, but the idea of caring for another human being, another life entirely dependent on him, was terrifying. The financial strain of buying the house had already stretched him thin; the added responsibility of a child seemed insurmountable. His carefully constructed world of comfort and security suddenly felt like a house of cards, ready to collapse at the slightest gust of wind.

He remembered the initial shock of Sira's announcement, the dismissive part of him that had instinctively questioned her motives. He'd briefly wondered if it was a manipulative tactic to control him, to push his friends and exes away. The thought still lingered, a shameful stain on his conscience. He recoiled at the cruelty of that initial thought, the way it reduced Sira's profound experience to a calculated scheme. The guilt gnawed at him, a relentless, bitter ache in his chest.

He'd always been conscious of maintaining friendships with his exes. He saw no harm in it, no betrayal. He valued those relationships, the connections forged over time. He believed in amicable breakups, in the possibility of maintaining healthy, respectful bonds even after a romantic relationship ended. But seeing the way Sira reacted to the easy camaraderie he shared with his exes, he began to understand how his casual approach could be misinterpreted. His easygoing nature, once a source of pride, now felt like a careless disregard for Sira's feelings.

His insecurity deepened as he considered the monumental changes that lay ahead. Fatherhood. Marriage. The sheer weight of these responsibilities was almost paralyzing. He'd envisioned a life with Sira, a comfortable existence built on mutual understanding and shared dreams. He'd always loved her; he couldn't deny the powerful, almost primal connection he felt. But this – this was different. This was a leap of faith into the unknown, a journey that required a level of commitment and selflessness he wasn't sure he was capable of.

He looked back at the ultrasound photo again, focusing on the tiny, undefined shape. He tried to connect with the life within, the growing presence that would soon join their world. A sudden wave of tenderness washed over him, a fragile hope amidst the storm of his anxieties. He could see a tiny hand, a tiny foot, a beating heart. And it was his. He was going to be a father.

He knew he needed to be better. He needed to be strong, reliable, and present for Sira. He needed to address his own insecurities, to confront his past, and to build a future that honored the depth and complexity of their love. He needed to trust Sira, to believe in her, and to understand that her anxieties weren't some calculated move to control him, but genuine fears born out of her own vulnerability and insecurity.

The brewing coffee finally finished, the machine emitting a satisfied sigh. The scent of coffee, rich and earthy, no longer mocked their silence, but instead offered a sense of normalcy, a grounding presence amidst the turbulence. He picked up two mugs, his hands steadier now. He needed to talk, to truly listen, to understand. He poured two steaming cups, the clinking of mugs a small, reassuring sound in the heavy silence. He offered one to Sira, his eyes conveying a silent plea for understanding, a promise of change. The dust motes continued their silent dance, but now, as he looked at Sira, he sensed a shift in the atmosphere, a tentative easing of the tension. The storm still raged within him, but a glimmer of hope, small yet undeniable, had begun to pierce the clouds. The journey ahead would be challenging, he knew, but for the first time, he felt a surge of determination, a quiet resolve to navigate the uncharted territory, not alone, but hand-in-hand with the woman he loved, and the child they were about to bring into the world. He reached for Sira's hand, his touch hesitant at first, then firm, a silent vow of commitment, a promise to face the future together, whatever it might bring. The ultrasound photo, lying between them, no longer felt like a judgment, but a symbol of the life they were about to create, a life that would test them, challenge them, and ultimately, strengthen their bond in ways they couldn't yet imagine.

Fears and Anxieties

The warmth of Keith's hand in hers offered a fragile comfort, but the tremor in his touch mirrored the turmoil churning within Sira. The quiet in the aftermath of their unspoken agreement felt heavy, pregnant with unspoken fears. As the coffee cooled, so did the initial wave of relief. The reality of her situation, a stark, unforgiving landscape, began to creep back in. It wasn't just the baby; it was everything. The weight of it all threatened to crush her.

The financial strain had been a constant undercurrent in their relationship, a low hum of anxiety that had now swelled into a deafening roar. Keith's impulsive decision to buy a house, while undeniably romantic, had amplified their precarious financial position. The mortgage payments loomed, a monstrous shadow over their future. Even with Keith's steady job, she felt the precariousness of their situation – a single unexpected expense, a sudden job loss, could topple their carefully constructed – and frankly, rather hastily built – world.

But it wasn't just the money. The fear of motherhood, vast and uncharted, terrified her. She'd always envisioned a different life, a life filled with travel, spontaneity, the freedom to pursue her own ambitions. Now, the future stretched before her, a seemingly endless expanse of diapers, sleepless nights, and the crushing responsibility of nurturing a tiny human being. Would she be a good mother? Was she even capable? The questions gnawed at her, relentless and unforgiving.

The weight of her anxieties wasn't solely tied to the practicalities of impending motherhood. The emotional toll was immense. The constant hormonal shifts left her a volatile cocktail of emotions—one minute brimming with overwhelming love, the next consumed by crippling anxiety. She missed the ease of their life before, a time of carefree spontaneity and effortless connection. Now, every decision felt laden with consequence, every interaction fraught with potential conflict. The simple act of choosing a restaurant could trigger a torrent of anxieties, an internal battle between practicality and desire, punctuated by a gnawing fear of disappointing Keith.

The presence of Keith's ex-girlfriends, the easy familiarity they shared, continued to prick at her. She knew, logically, that they were just friends, but the jealousy, a persistent green-eyed monster, gnawed at her self-esteem. Their presence was a constant reminder of a past she wasn't a part of, a shared history that excluded her. She saw the glances, the lingering smiles, the inside jokes, and her insecurities swelled. She battled against the irrationality of her feelings, recognizing them as her own vulnerabilities, yet struggling to quell the rising tide of self-doubt. Was she not enough? Was she simply not as good, as fun, as vibrant as those who had come before her?

The pregnancy itself felt like an added layer of complexity, a constant physical reminder of the changes reshaping her life, her body, her identity. The morning sickness, the fatigue, the constant awareness of the growing life within her – all of it amplified her anxieties. She was no longer just Sira; she was Sira, the pregnant girlfriend, the future mother, the woman grappling with the immense responsibility of building a life, a home, a family, in circumstances that felt increasingly tenuous.

She found herself constantly second-guessing herself, analyzing every word, every action, every emotion. Was she being too clingy? Too demanding? Was she inadvertently pushing Keith away with her worries? The fear of losing him, of shattering the fragile peace they had found, was a constant companion. The ultrasound photo, a tangible symbol of their future, sometimes felt more like a burden than a blessing. It represented not just a child, but the weight of their shared responsibilities, the uncertainties of their future, the anxieties that threatened to overwhelm her.

Evenings were the worst. The silence after Keith fell asleep felt amplified, the darkness a canvas upon which her worries painted themselves in vivid, terrifying detail. She'd lie awake, tracing the lines on her hand, a physical manifestation of her own uncertainties. She'd stare at the ceiling, watching the shadows dance, as her mind replayed every interaction, every conversation, searching for clues, for signs that she was failing, that she was losing him.

The therapy sessions she'd started offered some solace, a safe space to unpack her anxieties without judgment. Her therapist, a kind woman with wise eyes, listened patiently, helping Sira untangle the knotted threads of her worries. Slowly, painstakingly, Sira began to recognize the irrationality of some of her fears, to identify the patterns of her self-doubt. But the fear remained, a constant undercurrent beneath the surface of her thoughts, a whisper in the quiet moments.

She thought about her parents, their quiet strength in the face of adversity, their unwavering support. Yet, calling them felt daunting; her fears felt too immense, too personal, to share with them. The idea of revealing her anxieties, of confessing her insecurities, filled her with a wave of shame. She felt like a failure, unable to handle the demands of her life, the responsibilities of adulthood. How could she admit her struggles to the people who had always believed in her?

The simple act of leaving the house felt like an insurmountable task. The scrutiny, both real and imagined, felt overwhelming. Every glance, every whispered comment, was interpreted as judgment, a confirmation of her inadequacy. Even the simplest errands felt like high-stakes challenges, adding to the weight of the invisible pressure she felt.

Sleep offered little respite. Her dreams were filled with fragmented images, anxieties manifested in bizarre and unsettling scenarios. The exhaustion only deepened her anxieties, creating a vicious cycle that left her feeling trapped, overwhelmed, and utterly alone, even though Keith's hand often rested reassuringly on her stomach, a silent promise of support. His presence was a source of comfort, yet the deep well of her worries felt impossible to fully share. The fear that the depth of her anxieties would shatter their fragile peace kept a wall standing between them.

One morning, amidst the swirling vortex of her anxieties, a sudden, sharp realization struck her. This wasn't just about her fears; it was also about Keith's expectations, the unspoken pressures she felt to perform a role she wasn't yet ready for. She wasn't just a pregnant girlfriend; she was a soon-to-be mother, a partner navigating the complexities of a new home, a new life, a new financial landscape. She wasn't just failing; she was expected to succeed in all these aspects, perfectly, effortlessly.

The realization was both terrifying and liberating. It allowed her to see her anxieties not as personal failings, but as a reflection of the overwhelming pressure she was under. It wasn't just the pregnancy; it was the entire constellation of challenges swirling around her. She needed to communicate these fears, not to burden Keith, but to share the weight, to collaborate in navigating the unknown. She knew, instinctively, that the path to overcoming her anxieties lay not in suppressing them, but in sharing them, in seeking understanding and support.

The path to facing those fears would require courage, vulnerability, and a willingness to trust Keith not only with her fears but also with her own doubts about the future. The road ahead was undeniably challenging; yet, holding Keith's hand, feeling the gentle rhythm of the baby's movements inside her, she found a newfound strength, a growing resolve to face those challenges together. The uncertainty remained, but it was no longer an insurmountable obstacle. It was a shared journey, a path they would navigate, step by uncertain step, together.

Financial Strain and the House Purchase

The silence stretched, thick and heavy with unspoken anxieties. The gentle sway of the baby within Sira's belly was a stark contrast to the storm brewing in her mind. Keith's hand, still clasped in hers, felt warm and reassuring, yet the weight of their shared future pressed down on her, a suffocating blanket of uncertainty. The initial euphoria of their unspoken agreement – Keith's impulsive, yet deeply loving, decision to buy a house – was fading, replaced by the stark reality of their financial situation.

Their college romance had been idyllic, fueled by late-night study sessions, shared dreams, and the heady rush of young love. Money had been a distant worry, an abstract concept easily dismissed in the face of their passion. Now, facing the prospect of parenthood, the abstract had become brutally real. Sira's part-time job barely covered her expenses, and Keith, despite his promising career trajectory in software engineering, was still navigating the early stages of his professional life. His salary, while respectable, was hardly sufficient to cover the costs of a mortgage, diapers, baby food, and all the other expenses associated with raising a child.

The thought of the house itself, a symbol of Keith's commitment and love, now felt like a looming shadow. It wasn't just the mortgage payments, though those were undeniably daunting. It was the sheer scale of responsibility, the weight of providing for a family, the fear of failure. Sira's mind raced, calculating budgets, estimating expenses, and finding herself falling short at every turn. The charming little house Keith had found, with its quaint garden and sun-drenched rooms, seemed less like a haven and more like a gilded cage, a beautiful prison built on shaky financial foundations.

Keith, ever the optimist, brushed aside her concerns. "We'll figure it out, baby," he'd said, his voice laced with a confidence that Sira envied. He spoke of cutting back on expenses, of taking on extra work, of relying on family for support. His unwavering optimism, while comforting, also felt naive, a blissful ignorance of the harsh realities they faced. She loved his unwavering faith in their ability to overcome any obstacle, but beneath the surface, a chilling doubt gnawed at her. Could they really do this? Could they navigate this financial tightrope walk without losing their footing, without sacrificing their dreams, their relationship, their very selves?

The fear wasn't just about money. It was about the future, about the potential for strain on their relationship, about the pressure of providing for a child in a world that felt increasingly unforgiving. She envisioned endless nights spent worrying about bills, about the possibility of falling behind, about the weight of their debt slowly crushing them. It wasn't just about survival; it was about preserving the joy, the love, the easy laughter that defined their relationship before this wave of responsibility crashed over them. Would they emerge from this stronger, or would the relentless pressure break them?

The realization that Keith had made such a significant financial commitment – purchasing a house – without fully understanding the extent of their financial predicament sent a shiver down her spine. He'd been driven by love, by a desire to provide her and their unborn child with a stable and loving home. But that selfless act now loomed over her, a reminder of their precarious financial situation and the immense pressure they were under. Had he been too hasty? Had he overlooked the stark realities of their budget? The question lingered in the back of her mind, casting a long shadow over the initial joy and relief she felt upon hearing the news.

The weight of their financial struggles extended beyond the immediate concerns of paying the mortgage and providing for their child. It cast a pall over their dreams, threatening to smother the aspirations they had so carefully nurtured. Keith had envisioned a home filled with laughter, a haven where they could start their family and create a lifetime of memories. But now, that dream seemed clouded by the constant worry about money, about meeting their financial obligations, about the pressure of ensuring their child would never want for anything.

The fear of failure was a constant companion, a shadow that danced at the edges of her thoughts, growing larger and more menacing with each passing day. What if they couldn't afford it? What if they were forced to sell the house, giving up on the dream they had so eagerly embraced? What if the strain of their financial struggles caused irreparable damage to their relationship, the very foundation of their lives? These weren't idle worries; they were genuine concerns that gnawed at her, threatening to consume her with anxiety and self-doubt.

Sira found herself spending hours poring over financial documents, calculating budgets, and researching ways to cut expenses. She began to see the world through the lens of their financial limitations, constantly weighing the cost of every purchase, every outing, every small indulgence. The carefree joy that had once characterized her life was fading, replaced by a constant awareness of their precarious financial situation. The joy of expecting a child, a miracle they had both eagerly anticipated, was tinged with a pervasive anxiety about money and the future.

She felt guilty, for her anxieties casting a shadow on Keith's selfless gesture. He'd risked everything, mortgaged his future to give them a home, and here she was, consumed by doubt. She knew he was doing everything he could, and his efforts to support them were immeasurable. Yet, the sheer scale of their financial predicament was overwhelming, a weight that seemed to grow heavier with each passing day. The pressure to succeed, to provide, to make everything work, felt suffocating, threatening to crush her spirit.

The realization that she was letting her fears dictate her actions was a bitter pill to swallow. She knew she needed to find a way to balance her anxieties with Keith's unwavering optimism, to find a way to work together, to face their challenges with a united front. She knew it wouldn't be easy, and that there would be days when they would falter, when their fears would overwhelm them. But she also knew that they had to try, that they had to find a way to navigate these choppy waters together. The journey would be arduous, filled with setbacks and challenges, but the prize – a secure future for their family, a home filled with love and laughter – made the struggle worthwhile. The love they shared, the anticipation of their child's arrival, were anchors in the storm, providing the strength and resolve to weather the coming months, to find a way forward together. The house, a symbol of their commitment and their hopes for the future, would be the testament to their unwavering love and resilience. It would be their home, a place where they could build a life together, despite the financial hurdles that lay ahead.

Who are They

The next morning dawned bright and deceptively cheerful, a stark contrast to the tempest brewing inside Sira. She woke to the scent of freshly brewed coffee and the quiet hum of Keith's contented sighs beside her. He was already awake, his eyes closed, a peaceful smile gracing his lips. The sight should have been comforting, a testament to their love and shared future. Instead, a knot of anxiety tightened in her stomach. It was the unspoken things, the things left unsaid, that gnawed at her. The house, their future, the baby – all of it felt monumental, overwhelming. And then there were the ex-girlfriends.

The thought of them, the ghost of their presence, was a constant, unwelcome companion. She hadn't met them yet, but Keith had casually mentioned them, dropping names and anecdotes into conversations with a nonchalance that grated on Sira's nerves. There was Chloe, the artist with a bohemian spirit and a laugh that could fill a room. Keith had described her as his "best friend from college," a statement that hung heavy with unspoken implications. Then there was Olivia, the ambitious lawyer, sharp-witted and driven, whose ambition had seemingly outpaced their relationship. Keith had called her "incredibly talented" and "a force of nature," which, again, added fuel to Sira's growing insecurities. And finally, there was Layna, the quiet, thoughtful one, a musician who had inspired Keith's own musical leanings. Keith had referred to her as his "muse," leaving Sira with the uncomfortable feeling that a part of Keith still belonged to her.

These brief, seemingly insignificant mentions, each a carefully crafted sentence, had built a wall of apprehension in Sira's mind. She tried to dismiss her feelings as jealousy, as irrational insecurity brought on by pregnancy hormones and financial stress. But the unease lingered, a persistent shadow that stretched long and dark over their otherwise bright future.

Keith stirred, his eyes fluttering open. He smiled, a slow, sleepy curve of his lips that managed to calm the rising tide of her anxieties. "Morning, sleepyhead," he murmured, his voice thick with sleep. He pulled her closer, his arm wrapping around her waist, his body radiating warmth and comfort.

"Morning," she replied, trying to match his calm demeanor, but her voice betrayed her, a tremor betraying her inner turmoil. She decided to confront the elephant in the room.

"The ex-girlfriends," she began, her voice barely above a whisper. The words tasted bitter on her tongue.

Keith's smile faltered slightly. He sat up, pulling the covers around him. "What about them?" he asked, his voice gentle but laced with a hint of apprehension. He sensed the undercurrent of tension.

"You talk about them so casually," she explained, choosing her words carefully. "It makes me… uncomfortable."

He frowned, his brow furrowing in concentration. "I'm sorry, Sira. I didn't realize it bothered you. They're just…

friends. We've known each other for years. We've been through a lot together." He paused, searching for the right words. "Chloe helped me navigate my first year of college. Olivia helped me sort through some legal problems a few years back. And Layna… well, She and I were deeply into music. We shared a passion for creating music, which was a big part of our lives back then. But, those were years ago. And it's nothing you have to worry about, truly, because our relationship, our love and our baby— that's all that matters now."

His explanation, though sincere, did little to quell Sira's anxieties. The casual nature of his words, the easy way he spoke of their shared history, only intensified her unease. Years of shared experiences, inside jokes, memories etched into the fabric of his life – these were things she wasn't a part of. She was the new addition, the pregnant girlfriend who had arrived to change the course of the story. It felt like she was stepping into a life that was already established and rich, with her own history only beginning now, whilst Keith's continued into the present and future.

"I know they're just friends," she replied, her voice softer now, but the underlying tension remained. "But it's hard, you know? It's hard to feel like I'm the only one in your life now, or the only one of importance, especially when I'm already feeling overwhelmed and insecure about everything else."

He reached for her hand, his touch gentle but firm. "Sira, I understand. I truly do. But you are the most important person in my life. You and our baby. My past relationships are just that – past. They don't define who I am now, or who I want to be. I want to build a future with you, with our child. You're the woman I love. Everything else pales in comparison." His eyes held hers, their depths reflecting a sincerity that she couldn't deny. Yet, the doubt lingered, a seed of insecurity planted deep within her heart.

The conversation, though seemingly resolved, left a residue of unease. The image of Keith surrounded by his ex-girlfriends, a circle of laughter and shared history, haunted her thoughts throughout the day. She found herself scrutinizing his every interaction, imagining hidden meanings and unspoken connections. Even his simple gestures, the way he smiled or laughed, seemed colored by the ghosts of his past relationships.

That evening, as Keith prepared dinner, she found herself observing him from a distance. The casual way he called Chloe on the phone to chat, the familiarity in his voice, a quick, easy joke shared— all felt foreign, intrusive. The lighthearted conversation highlighted the difference in their histories. His world extended beyond their present.

Later that night, as they lay in bed, the baby stirring within Sira, she realized that her anxieties were not simply about Keith's past. They were about her own insecurities, her own fears of inadequacy, her own fear of not being enough. The financial pressures, the pregnancy anxieties – all of these factors were magnifying her fears and insecurities, causing her to project those anxieties onto Keith's past relationships.

She needed to address these feelings, not only for herself but for the sake of her relationship with Keith. She knew that she needed to find a way to confront her fears, to find a way to trust him and build a solid foundation for their future, not just for them as a couple, but for the future of their child. She needed to learn to separate the anxieties of the present and the ghosts of the past. The future, with its many uncertainties and challenges, lay before them, and it was a future she wanted to share with Keith, wholeheartedly and unconditionally.

The realization settled like a calm after a storm, not eliminating the anxieties, but soothing the intensity. The next morning, she approached Keith with newfound resolve, ready to tackle the challenges ahead, one step at a time.

Chapter 2:

Therapy Sessions

The sterile scent of antiseptic and the muted beige of the waiting room did little to soothe Sira's frayed nerves. Her hands, usually so graceful in their movements, fidgeted nervously in her lap. The weight of her pregnancy, the ever-present shadow of Keith's ex-girlfriends, and the gnawing insecurity that threatened to consume her had finally pushed her to seek professional help. She'd found Dr. Anya Sharma through a recommendation from a friend, a woman who'd navigated a similar storm of anxieties during her own pregnancy.

Dr. Sharma's office was surprisingly warm and inviting, a stark contrast to the impersonal waiting area. Soft lighting, a comfortable armchair, and a collection of calming nature photographs created a space that felt less like a clinical setting and more like a sanctuary. Dr. Sharma herself was a calming presence, her warm smile and gentle eyes instantly putting Sira at ease.

"So, Sira," Dr. Sharma began, her voice a soft melody, "tell me what brings you in today."

Sira hesitated, the floodgates of her anxieties threatening to burst open. She took a deep breath, trying to organize her chaotic thoughts. "It's… everything, I think," she finally managed, her voice barely above a whisper. "The pregnancy, the relationship with Keith… it all feels so overwhelming."

She launched into a detailed account of her anxieties, starting with the initial shock and subsequent fear of the pregnancy announcement. She described Keith's initial skepticism, his quiet doubts, the way he'd interpreted her news as a calculated move to create distance between him and his exes. She confessed her own self-doubt, the fear that he might be right, that she'd inadvertently sabotaged their relationship. The conversation flowed easily, a mixture of tears and hesitant confessions.

Dr. Sharma listened patiently, offering occasional nods and insightful prompts. She didn't interrupt or judge, allowing Sira to unravel her tangled emotions at her own pace. As Sira spoke, she realized the depth of her insecurities weren't solely tied to Keith's past relationships. They stemmed from deeper-rooted issues, insecurities that had been with her long before Keith entered her life.

"I've always felt… inadequate," she admitted, her voice cracking. "Not good enough. In school, I always felt overshadowed by other girls, prettier, smarter, more popular. Even with Keith, I constantly compare myself to his exes. Am I as funny? As attractive? As interesting?"

Dr. Sharma's response was gentle but firm. "Sira, it's natural to feel insecure sometimes, especially during such a significant life transition. But these feelings of inadequacy are not reflections of your true worth. Comparing yourself to others is a recipe for unhappiness. Each person has unique qualities and strengths. You are not defined by how you measure up to others."

The sessions continued over several weeks, each one peeling back another layer of Sira's emotional baggage. They explored her childhood, her relationship with her parents, and the patterns of insecurity that had developed throughout her life. Dr. Sharma helped her identify her coping mechanisms – excessive cleaning, isolating herself from friends, and engaging in self-criticism. She gently challenged Sira's negative self-talk, replacing it with more compassionate and realistic self-assessments.

One session focused on her relationship with Keith. Dr. Sharma helped Sira articulate her needs and desires more effectively, showing her how to communicate those needs without resorting to accusations or resentment. She learned to identify the triggers that amplified her anxieties – Keith's late-night phone calls with his friends, casual mentions of his exes, even the innocent laughter that sometimes echoed from his phone conversations. Dr. Sharma helped her understand that these triggers weren't necessarily evidence of Keith's infidelity or lack of love, but rather manifestations of her own unresolved fears.

"It's important to differentiate between your fears and reality, Sira," Dr. Sharma explained. "Your anxieties stem from your past experiences and your own insecurities. But they are not necessarily indicators of Keith's feelings or intentions. Open, honest communication will help you address these anxieties collaboratively with Keith. Instead of focusing on potential threats, concentrate on building trust and security in your relationship."

Through therapy, Sira gained a newfound self-awareness, understanding the root causes of her anxieties and learning healthier ways to cope. She learned to communicate her feelings to Keith more effectively, expressing her concerns without resorting to blame or accusations. Their conversations became more open and honest, and she felt a growing sense of comfort and security in their relationship, even amidst the challenges of pregnancy and the presence of Keith's ex-girlfriends.

The therapy helped Sira embrace her pregnancy with a renewed sense of confidence. Instead of succumbing to fear and insecurity, she began focusing on the joy and excitement of motherhood, attending prenatal classes and eagerly preparing for the arrival of her child. She learned to celebrate her own strengths and qualities, recognizing her resilience, her empathy, and her unwavering love for Keith. The insecurity still lingered sometimes, a faint whisper in the back of her mind, but it no longer held the power to consume her.

Her relationship with Keith also underwent a transformation. He began to understand the depth of her anxieties, realizing that her concerns weren't about manipulating him but about protecting her own emotional well-being. He made conscious efforts to reassure her, offering support and understanding. He listened more attentively, and learned to recognize the subtle signs of her anxieties. He even started limiting his late-night calls with his friends and avoided casual discussions about his exes, recognizing that these actions unknowingly fueled Sira's insecurity.

The sessions weren't a magic cure; they were a tool. Therapy provided Sira with the skills and insights she needed to navigate the complexities of her life, to confront her insecurities, and to build a stronger, healthier relationship with Keith. It was a journey of self-discovery, of confronting her past, and of learning to embrace the present with a newfound sense of confidence and self-worth. The path wasn't always smooth, but with Dr. Sharma's guidance, Sira felt equipped to face the challenges ahead, armed with a newfound understanding of herself and a stronger relationship with Keith. The weight of her anxieties, once a crushing burden, gradually began to lift, replaced by a sense of hope and anticipation for the future, a future filled with the promise of motherhood and a love that was slowly but surely becoming more resilient, more mature, and more authentically theirs. The journey was far from over, but with each passing session, Sira felt herself stepping closer towards a healthier, more secure version of herself, ready to embrace whatever lay ahead.

The Farther we Grow

The newfound sense of calm Sira had cultivated in therapy began to fray at the edges. The chasm between her anxieties and Keith's perceived nonchalance was growing, a silent canyon carved by unspoken words and misinterpreted gestures. It started subtly, with a missed call here, a delayed text there. Keith, absorbed in his demanding job as a software engineer, often worked late, leaving Sira feeling neglected, her worries amplified by the solitude of the large house he'd bought for them – a house that felt less like a haven and more like a monument to their growing distance.

One evening, Keith arrived home late, the scent of takeout clinging to his clothes. He'd promised to help Sira assemble the baby's crib, a task she'd been dreading due to the complicated instructions. "Sorry, honey," he mumbled, dropping his bag onto the floor with a thud. "Long day. We can do the crib tomorrow."

To Sira, this felt like another dismissal, a careless disregard for her needs. The exhaustion clinging to her bones, the physical discomfort of pregnancy, and the emotional toll of her anxieties all coalesced into a wave of resentment. "Tomorrow?" she replied, her voice sharper than she intended. "Tomorrow is always the promise, Keith. But tomorrow never comes."

Keith looked up, startled by the icy tone in her voice. He hadn't meant to dismiss her; he was simply tired, overwhelmed by work pressures. His attempt at an apology – a clumsy, heartfelt murmur about his long hours and the demanding project deadlines – only served to further widen the gulf between them. He didn't understand the depth of her frustration, the cumulative effect of small slights and unmet expectations. To him, it felt like an unwarranted attack, a criticism of his dedication to providing for them.

He saw his late nights and hard work as proof of his love, a tangible expression of his commitment to their future. But to Sira, it felt like a lack of presence, a failure to acknowledge the emotional labor of pregnancy and the anxieties that consumed her.

Their communication styles clashed dramatically. Sira, a creative writer with a penchant for emotional expressiveness, communicated through nuanced tones, subtle gestures, and unspoken expectations. Keith, a pragmatic logician, valued direct, straightforward communication. He found Sira's indirect hints and subtle criticisms frustratingly vague, preferring clear articulation of needs and concerns. He didn't understand her need for constant reassurance, for the small acts of affection that would alleviate her anxieties. He believed his actions spoke louder than words; his provision of a house, his hard work, his unwavering commitment to the future.

The incident with the crib became a microcosm of their larger problems. What started as a simple missed opportunity to spend time together escalated into a full-blown argument, fueled by unspoken resentments and misinterpretations. Sira accused Keith of being insensitive to her pregnancy struggles, of prioritizing his work over their relationship. Keith, in turn, felt unjustly accused, his efforts to provide for them minimized and dismissed. They talked past each other, their words ricocheting off the unspoken anxieties and unmet expectations that had silently accumulated between them.

The following days were marked by a palpable tension. The house, once a symbol of their shared future, now felt like a cold, empty space between them. Sira found herself retreating into herself, her anxieties worsening with each passing day. She started spending more time in her therapy sessions, grappling with the communication breakdown, the growing distance, and the gnawing fear that their relationship was unraveling.

Dr. Sharma listened patiently, offering insights into their differing communication styles and the impact of their personality differences on their relationship. She encouraged Sira to articulate her needs more directly, to express her anxieties without resorting to indirect accusations. She also suggested that Keith work on actively listening to Sira's concerns, validating her feelings even if he didn't fully understand them. The therapist stressed the importance of empathy and understanding, of learning to communicate not just what they wanted to say, but what the other person needed to hear.

Sira, armed with Dr. Sharma's advice, attempted a different approach. One evening, she sat Keith down, her voice calm but firm. She explained her anxieties, the cumulative effect of his late nights and the lack of shared moments. She spoke not of accusations, but of her needs: a little more attention, a little more reassurance, a little more help with the mundane tasks that were becoming increasingly difficult with her pregnancy. She spoke not of his failures, but of her fears and insecurities. She expressed her love and her hope for their future, emphasizing the need for them to work together to bridge the growing gap between them.

Keith, surprised by her direct and vulnerable approach, listened intently. He listened not just to the words, but to the unspoken anxieties in her tone, the desperation in her eyes. He finally understood the depth of her struggles, the weight of her emotional burden. He confessed his own fears, his anxieties about providing for them, his inability to balance his demanding job with the emotional needs of his pregnant partner. He acknowledged his shortcomings, his failures to understand her unspoken anxieties, and his tendency to express his love through material provision rather than emotional support.

The conversation was difficult, raw, and emotionally charged, but it was also a turning point. It was a shared vulnerability, a mutual acknowledgment of their failures, and a commitment to build a stronger, more communicative foundation for their relationship. They agreed to set aside dedicated time each day to connect, to talk, to share not just the logistics of their lives, but also their emotions, their fears, and their hopes. They started attending couples therapy, a step that further strengthened their resolve to overcome the growing distance and the constant miscommunications that threatened to tear them apart.

The path to healing wasn't easy. There were still moments of frustration, of missed cues, of misunderstandings. But now, armed with a newfound understanding of each other's needs, they were better equipped to navigate the complexities of their relationship. They were learning to bridge the gap between their different communication styles, to find common ground in their shared love and their commitment to their future together. The house still stood as a symbol of their shared life, but now, it felt less like an imposing structure and more like a home, a haven slowly being built on a foundation of trust, understanding, and open communication. The journey was far from over, but with each step, they moved closer to a more resilient, more mature, and more deeply loving partnership. The anxieties remained, but they were now facing them together, side by side, learning to communicate, to empathize, and to build a future filled not just with material provisions, but with the invaluable currency of shared understanding and unwavering love.

Reconciliation

The silence in the house was thick, heavy with the unspoken accusations hanging between them. Sira's quiet withdrawal had become a wall, a fortress built of hurt feelings and unmet needs. Keith, finally realizing the depth of his missteps, felt a cold dread settle in his stomach. He'd thought his actions – buying the house, providing financially – were enough to prove his love, his commitment. But he'd failed to see that material gestures were meaningless without the emotional currency of understanding and reassurance.

He started small. He made her breakfast, not the usual grab-and-go cereal, but fluffy pancakes, perfectly browned, accompanied by fresh berries and a steaming cup of her favorite tea. He'd even remembered the extra honey she liked. He left it on the kitchen island, a silent offering, a tangible expression of his remorse. When she emerged, her eyes still clouded with a sadness that cut him to the core, he braced himself.

"Good morning," he said softly, his voice a little rough around the edges. The silence stretched, thin and taut. He waited, his heart thudding against his ribs, for her reaction. He expected anger, resentment, maybe even tears. Instead, Sira simply nodded, her gaze lingering on breakfast. A small, almost imperceptible sigh escaped her lips.

He didn't push it. He knew that forcing connection would be counterproductive. Instead, he went about his morning routine, deliberately keeping his movements quiet, respecting the fragile space that existed between them. He made sure to be present, to offer a hand without being intrusive, to listen without interrupting. He noticed the way she cradled her stomach, the gentle caress, a silent conversation between mother and child.

Later that day, after a long and emotionally draining afternoon at work, he came home with a bouquet of her favorite lilies, their fragrant blossoms a silent apology. This time, Sira's response was a little warmer. She took the flowers, her fingers brushing his as she accepted them. A small, hesitant smile played on her lips.

"Thank you," she whispered, her voice barely audible. It was a start.

That evening, he sat beside her on the couch, the television a muted background hum. He didn't try to initiate a conversation, instead simply offering his presence, his silent support. He held her hand, her fingers small and delicate in his. He felt the slight tremor in her touch, the subtle tension in her body. He knew she was still hurt, still struggling with her insecurities, but he also sensed a flicker of hope, a tiny spark of reconnection.

He began to read books about pregnancy and postnatal depression, desperate to understand the hormonal shifts and emotional turmoil she was going through. He discovered the profound physical and emotional changes that transformed a woman's life, changes he hadn't fully appreciated before. He learned about the anxieties that often accompanied pregnancy, the fear of the unknown, the vulnerability that made her feel so exposed.

He also researched communication techniques, learning to listen actively, to reflect her feelings without judgment, to validate her experiences, even when he didn't fully understand them. He discovered the importance of empathetic listening, understanding that her concerns weren't irrational, but a consequence of the intense physical and emotional changes she was undergoing.

His attempts weren't always perfect. He still stumbled, still missing steps. There were times when he reverted to old habits, when he tried to fix her problems instead of listening to her concerns. There were moments when his frustration flared, when his own insecurities threatened to overwhelm him.

One such occasion occurred when they were discussing the upcoming baby shower. Sira had meticulously planned the event, envisioned the décor, the food, the guest list. But Keith, overwhelmed by the pressure of work and the looming responsibilities of fatherhood, had brushed off her suggestions. His dismissive attitude ignited a firestorm in Sira.

"You're not even trying," she accused, her voice sharp with hurt and disappointment. Tears welled up in her eyes. "This is important to me, Keith. It's our baby."

He recoiled, hurt by the accusation. He tried to defend himself, to explain his exhaustion, but his words came out clumsy and insensitive. He realized, with a jolt of self-awareness, that he had, once again, failed to see things from her perspective.

"I'm sorry," he said, his voice soft but sincere. "I messed up. I didn't realize how much this meant to you."

He listened, really listened, this time. He let her express her emotions without interruption, without trying to fix or minimize her feelings. He simply let her talk, letting her tears flow freely. He held her close, his arms wrapping around her, offering comfort and solace. He realized that sometimes, all she needed was to be heard, to be understood, to feel his unwavering support.

He started to actively involve himself in the planning of the baby shower, asking about her preferences, offering suggestions, sharing the workload. He even surprised her by taking on the task of coordinating the guest list, meticulously reaching out to family and friends. This time, it wasn't just a gesture, but a sincere effort to show her that he valued her feelings, that he was committed to their future together.

The journey wasn't easy. There were still moments of doubt, of fear, of insecurity. But through it all, he persevered. He learned to communicate effectively, to listen intently, to truly see her, not just as his girlfriend, but as a woman going through an intense physical and emotional transformation. He learned that love wasn't just about providing for her materially, but also about nurturing her emotionally, validating her fears, and celebrating her joys.

He learned that genuine connection required understanding, empathy, and a willingness to put her needs first. The house they shared still stood as a symbol of their commitment, but it was no longer a cold monument to their distance, but rather a haven slowly being built on the foundation of mutual understanding, unwavering love, and the promise of a bright future together. The anxieties lingered, but now, they faced them hand in hand, committed to building a strong and enduring relationship, a testament to their love and their resilience. The path ahead was still uncertain, filled with the challenges that accompany parenthood and navigating the complexities of adult life. But with each passing day, their bond deepened, strengthened by their shared experiences, their unwavering commitment, and their growing understanding of each other's hearts.

There She Is

The first time Chloe mentioned the housewarming party, Sira felt a familiar knot tighten in her stomach. Chloe, one of Keith's ex-girlfriends, was a bubbly, perpetually cheerful presence in his life, the kind of woman who seemed to effortlessly radiate sunshine. Sira, however, found herself bristling at the thought of another woman, one who had shared intimacy with Keith, stepping into their newly established home. It wasn't that she disliked Chloe; it was the underlying current of insecurity that Chloe's presence, and the presence of other exes, stirred within her. This wasn't just about sharing a space; it was about sharing Keith.

Keith, oblivious to the turmoil brewing inside Sira, was excitedly planning the party. He saw it as a way to integrate Sira into his life, to show her that his past relationships held no bearing on their future. He'd carefully explained to his exes the significance of this event, emphasizing Sira's importance and his commitment to their relationship. Yet,

Sira couldn't shake the feeling that she was walking into a lion's den, surrounded by women who knew Keith better than she did, women who held a piece of his past, a past that felt both distant and intimately close, simultaneously.

The party itself was a kaleidoscope of awkward smiles and forced pleasantries. Chloe, true to form, was warm and welcoming, showering Sira with compliments and engaging her in light conversation. But beneath the veneer of cordiality, Sira felt a subtle tension, a competitive edge that prickled her skin. It wasn't overtly hostile; it was more of a silent undercurrent, a subtle vying for attention, a silent assertion of their shared history with Keith.

Another ex-girlfriend, Sarah, arrived later. Sarah was different from Chloe; she was quieter, more reserved, her eyes holding a depth that suggested a more complex history with Keith. Their exchange was minimal, polite but distant. Sira felt a sense of unease watching Keith effortlessly navigate between the two women, his charm and ease making her feel even more out of place, a stranger in her own home.

The evening progressed with a flurry of forced laughter and strained conversations. Sira found herself retreating into herself, observing the interactions between Keith and his exes with a growing sense of disquiet. The ease with which he transitioned between them, the comfortable familiarity of their interactions, fueled the fire of her insecurities. It wasn't that she doubted Keith's commitment; it was the unfamiliar territory of sharing him, even in a platonic way, that made her heart pound. She felt like an intruder in a world she wasn't sure she belonged to.

Later, as the party wound down, and the last guests departed, Sira confronted Keith. The words tumbled out, a torrent of anxieties and insecurities she'd held back for too long. She didn't blame him for his past relationships; she blamed herself for feeling so inadequate, so overshadowed by the ghosts of his past.

Keith listened patiently, his expression shifting from surprise to understanding. He held her close, his touch calming, reassuring. He explained, once again, that his past relationships were just that – past. He emphasized that Sira was his present, his future, and that his love for her was absolute. But his words, while heartfelt, did little to completely alleviate her anxieties. The seed of doubt had been planted, and it was stubbornly refusing to disappear.

The following days were a slow process of rebuilding trust and reassurance. Keith made a conscious effort to address Sira's anxieties. He spent extra time with her, making her feel cherished and loved. He made sure to involve her in decision-making processes, both big and small, so she felt like an equal partner. He began to understand the depth of her insecurity, recognizing that his past relationships, no matter how amicable, were a trigger for her anxieties about their present. He started to acknowledge and validate her feelings, instead of dismissing them as irrational or unnecessary.

He also involved Sira in conversations about his past relationships, not in a way that was invasive or disrespectful, but in a way that helped her understand the context. He shared stories, anecdotes, and perspectives, helping to paint a fuller picture of his past. This helped Sira understand that his relationships with his exes were distinct, and that his feelings for her were different, deeper, and more profound.

But the healing process wasn't immediate. Sira found herself frequently reviewing conversations, analyzing interactions, searching for hidden meanings that weren't there. She over-analyzed texts, phone calls, and even casual social media interactions. This obsessive behavior became a pattern, a vicious cycle that was fueled by her fears and insecurities.

One day, Keith came home from work with a thoughtful gift – a framed photograph of them together, a candid shot that captured their shared laughter. He had it professionally printed and framed. "I wanted you to have something to remind you that this is our story now, Sira," he said gently. His words, coupled with the simple gesture, spoke volumes. He wasn't trying to erase his past; he was trying to build a secure and loving future with her, a future where she felt loved, valued, and completely secure.

Sira, understanding his intent, accepted the gift with a grateful smile. It wasn't just a photograph; it was a tangible representation of his unwavering commitment and love. This small action symbolized a turning point in their relationship, a shift towards a deeper, more secure bond. The lingering insecurities were still present, like faint shadows on a sunny day, but they no longer dominated their relationship. They were learning to navigate them together, to communicate openly and honestly, to build a strong foundation for their future.

The challenge remained, however, in Sira's struggle to fully embrace this newfound security. The anxieties, though lessened, still surfaced unexpectedly. A casual mention of a shared memory between Keith and Chloe, a simple phone call between Keith and Sarah, were enough to spark the embers of insecurity. Sira recognized this pattern, realizing that her anxieties stemmed not solely from Keith's past relationships but also from her own past experiences and insecurities.

One evening, while talking to Keith, she admitted her struggle to fully let go of her jealousy. Keith listened attentively, validating her feelings and offering his support. It was in this moment that Sira realized that her concerns weren't about Keith's exes per se, but rather a reflection of her own internal conflicts and a fear of abandonment. She decided to seek professional help.

Therapy sessions proved to be immensely helpful. Through guided conversations, Sira delved into her past experiences and identified the root causes of her insecurities. She learned to recognize her thought patterns and challenge her negative beliefs. The therapist helped her understand that jealousy, while a natural emotion, often stems from personal insecurities and a lack of self-worth. The therapy sessions provided Sira with the tools to manage her anxiety and build a stronger sense of self-esteem. She began to understand that her worth wasn't defined by Keith's past or present relationships, but rather by her own inherent qualities and strengths.

As Sira started to address her internal struggles, her anxieties about Keith's ex-girlfriends gradually diminished. The interactions, once fraught with tension, became more comfortable, even friendly. She started to see Chloe and Sarah not as rivals, but as individuals in Keith's past who had contributed to shaping the man he is today. She understood that Keith's past experiences, both positive and negative, had helped him grow and become a better partner to her.

Keith, too, underwent a transformation. He learned to be more attuned to Sira's emotional needs. He became more proactive in assuring her of his love and commitment, not just through grand gestures, but through small, everyday acts of kindness and affection. He understood that true love wasn't about eliminating insecurities but about navigating them together, supporting each other through thick and thin.

Their relationship wasn't perfect, of course. There were still moments of vulnerability, moments of doubt, moments of insecurity. But these moments were met with empathy, understanding, and a commitment to work through them together. The presence of Keith's ex-girlfriends was no longer a source of significant tension or anxiety; it was simply a part of their shared history, a part that contributed to the rich tapestry of their evolving love story. The house, once a symbol of Sira's anxieties, now stood as a testament to their resilience, their love, and their unwavering commitment to building a strong and enduring future together. The journey was far from over, but they were facing it, hand in hand, ready to conquer any challenges that lie ahead. They were learning that love wasn't about erasing the past, but about creating a beautiful future, together.

Growing Isolation

The nausea was relentless, a constant, churning tide that threatened to pull her under. It wasn't just the morning sickness; it was a deeper malaise, a pervasive loneliness that clung to her like a second skin. The house, once a symbol of hope and a new beginning, now felt cavernous and empty, the silence amplifying the anxieties that gnawed at her. Keith was working late, again. He'd promised to spend more time with her, to be more present as the pregnancy progressed, but promises felt flimsy, like the delicate China teacups she'd carefully unpacked, fragile and easily broken.

She wandered from room to room, each space echoing with the absence of his presence. The nursery, still largely undecorated, felt like a cruel reminder of the impending future, a future she wasn't entirely sure she was ready for. The thought of motherhood, once a source of overwhelming joy, now felt like a burden, a weight pressing down on her chest, suffocating her. She longed for his comforting touch, the warmth of his body beside her, but the space beside her in bed remained cold and empty.

The silence was punctuated only by the rhythmic tick-tock of the grandfather clock in the hallway, each second a tiny hammer blow against her already frayed nerves. She tried to read, to lose herself in the pages of a book, but the words blurred, the stories failing to capture her attention. Her mind raced, a relentless carousel of anxieties, fears, and insecurities. She thought about her therapist, Dr. Anya Sharma, and their last session. Dr. Sharma had gently probed her feelings about the pregnancy, about Keith, about her own shifting identity.

"It's okay to feel overwhelmed, Sira," Dr. Sharma had said, her voice calm and soothing, a stark contrast to the tempest raging within Sira. "This is a huge life change, and it's natural to experience a range of emotions, even conflicting ones."

But the conflicting emotions felt like a battleground within her, a warzone where hope and despair fought for dominance. She loved Keith, she truly did, but the distance that had grown between them was palpable, a chasm that seemed to widen with each passing day. His preoccupation with work, his fleeting moments of exasperation at her emotional volatility, his continued contact with his exes—it all fed the insidious whispers of doubt that gnawed at her self-esteem.

She pulled out her phone, her fingers hovering over Keith's contact. She wanted to call him, to hear his voice, to feel reassured, but fear held her back. What if he was too busy? What if he snapped at her again? The fear of rejection was a constant companion, a shadow that followed her everywhere.

She scrolled through her social media, her thumb scrolling through images of happy couples, pregnant women glowing with joy, families celebrating milestones. Each picture felt like a tiny pinprick, a reminder of her own feelings of inadequacy, her own sense of isolation. She felt like an outsider looking in, watching others live lives she longed for, lives filled with unwavering support, unconditional love, and shared joy. Her reality was a stark contrast—a landscape of uncertainty, punctuated by moments of fear and loneliness.

The thought of her high school boyfriend, Noah, suddenly surfaced in her mind. His surprise visit a few weeks ago had been jarring, a sudden ripple in the already turbulent waters of her life. Noah, with his easy charm and genuine concern, had seen through her cover of strength, sensing the vulnerability beneath. He'd listened, offering words of support and understanding, a stark contrast to Keith's often distracted and impatient responses.

The memory of Noah's embrace, his comforting presence, sparked a pang of longing, a wistful yearning for a simpler time, a time before the complexities of adult life, before the anxieties of pregnancy, before the insecurities that threatened to consume her. It wasn't that she wanted to be with Noah; it was the stark contrast between his warmth and Keith's current distance that made her heart ache. It highlighted the growing gap between her and Keith, the lack of genuine connection that had become so apparent in recent weeks.

The afternoon stretched into evening, and still, Keith hadn't called. The silence in the house was deafening, each creak of the floorboards, each rustle of the wind against the windows, amplifying the emptiness in her heart. She stared out at the darkening sky, the city lights twinkling like distant stars, unreachable and unattainable. She felt a desperate yearning for connection, for someone to understand, to share the burden of her anxieties.

She found herself wandering towards the nursery again, touching the soft fabric of a tiny onesie she'd bought. Tears welled in her eyes, tears not just of sadness, but also of fear. Fear for the future, fear for the relationship, fear for herself. Would she be a good mother? Would Keith be there for her? Would they make it through this? The weight of these questions, unanswered and unspoken, felt crushing.

She picked up her phone again, her hand trembling slightly as she dialed Dr. Sharma's number. She needed to talk, to unburden herself, to find some semblance of solace in the midst of the storm raging within her. The therapist's calm voice on the other end was a lifeline, a beacon in the darkness, offering a promise of understanding and support. As she poured out her anxieties, her fears, and her growing sense of isolation, she felt a glimmer of hope, a tiny spark in the vast emptiness. The road ahead was still uncertain, but for the first time in days, she felt a sense of calm, a fragile peace that whispered the possibility of healing, of reconciliation, of a future where she wasn't alone.

The call ended, but the sense of calm lingered. She decided to take a long, hot bath, the steam rising around her like a gentle embrace. As she lay submerged, the water washing away the physical and emotional grime of the day, she began to feel a shift within herself, a gradual easing of tension. The isolation still lingered, but it no longer felt so absolute, so crushing. She had taken the first step, the most important step, towards acknowledging her feelings, towards reaching out for help. It wasn't a cure, but it was a beginning, a promise of something better, something stronger, something more resilient.

Later that evening, Keith finally arrived home, his face etched with fatigue and worry. He saw the subtle shift in Sira's demeanor, the quiet strength that had replaced the earlier despair. He saw the lingering sadness, but he also saw a flicker of hope. He pulled her into a hug, holding her close, letting her feel the warmth of his body against hers, a silent promise of support and understanding. It wasn't a grand gesture, not a sudden resolution to their problems, but it was a start. A beginning of a renewed effort, a fresh attempt at bridging the gap that had widened between them. The road ahead would still be challenging, but as she rested her head on his chest, feeling his heartbeat against her own, Sira felt a flicker of confidence, a tentative belief that perhaps, just perhaps, they could navigate the complexities of their relationship, together. The journey would be long, but at least she wasn't facing it alone. The isolation, while still present, felt less overwhelming, less suffocating. There was hope, a fragile, tentative hope, that things might get better. The future remained uncertain, but tonight, for tonight, Sira found solace in the warmth of Keith's embrace, a tangible counterpoint to the chilling loneliness that had threatened to consume her.

Chapter 3:

The Heat

The air in the newly purchased house, a space Keith had envisioned as a haven, crackled with tension. It wasn't the quiet, comfortable tension of a couple anticipating a child; this was a volatile, simmering anger that threatened to boil over. The argument started subtly, a misplaced grocery item escalating into a snippy exchange about Keith's late nights with his friends, a pattern that had become increasingly frequent since the house purchase. Sira, her pregnancy now clearly visible under a loose-fitting sweater, felt a familiar pang of insecurity. The house, meant to be a symbol of security, felt more like a gilded cage, trapping her in a cycle of anxieties.

"It's just dinner, Keith," she said, her voice tight with suppressed frustration, "But it's another example. Another night out with the guys, another night you're not here." The unspoken accusation hung heavy in the air: another night spent with them , his ex-girlfriends included. She hadn't explicitly mentioned them, but the implication was clear, a silent, bitter undercurrent to every disagreement.

Keith sighed, rubbing his temples with a weary hand. He'd been trying so hard. The house, the relentless job hunting, the constant worry about providing for Sira and their child – it all weighed heavily on him. He felt utterly depleted, stretched thin to the breaking point. "I'm trying, Sira," he said defensively. "I'm trying to make this work. I bought this house, didn't I?" He gestured around the sparsely furnished living room, a stark reminder of their financial struggles.

"Buying a house doesn't magically solve everything," Sira retorted, her voice rising. "It's not about the house,

Keith. It's about you. You're spending so much time with your friends, your exes , that you're barely here for me." The words spilled out, raw and unfiltered, fueled by exhaustion and mounting fear. The pregnancy hormones, she knew, didn't help matters, but that didn't invalidate her feelings.

Keith flinched. The accusation, though implied before, now hit him with the force of a physical blow. He'd tried to explain, to reassure her that his friendships were innocent, that he valued her above all else, but his attempts had fallen on increasingly deaf ears. "Don't start with that again," he snapped, regret lacing his tone the instant the words left his mouth. "You're twisting things. It's not like that."

"Is it?" Sira challenged, her eyes blazing. The fight wasn't just about late nights and misplaced groceries; it was about the simmering resentment that had been building since the pregnancy announcement. It was about Keith's lingering doubts, his initial suspicion that the pregnancy was a calculated move. It was about the inherent insecurities that threatened to unravel their relationship. "Is it, Keith? Because I feel like you're constantly choosing them over me."

The words hung in the air, thick with unspoken anxieties. Keith looked at Sira, truly saw her – the exhaustion etched on her face, the worry lines around her eyes, the fragile beauty of a woman carrying his child. He saw the vulnerability he'd so often failed to acknowledge, dismissing her fears as irrational, melodramatic, or a manipulative tactic to control him. He'd been so focused on proving his worth, on providing for her, that he'd neglected to truly listen, to understand the depths of her apprehension. He'd let his own insecurities cloud his judgment, building a wall between them instead of bridging the gap.

He knew, in that moment, that he'd failed her. He'd failed to adequately address her concerns, to reassure her, to support her. The weight of his mistakes settled upon him like a physical burden.

The argument escalated further, veering wildly from misplaced groceries to Keith's ex-girlfriends to the financial pressures that weighed heavily on them. Sira accused him of prioritizing his social life over his responsibilities, of not understanding the emotional and physical toll of pregnancy, of being selfish and insensitive. Keith, overwhelmed by the accusations and his own guilt, countered with his own frustrations: the pressure of providing for them, the stress of juggling a new job and a strained relationship, his feelings of inadequacy.

The words were like weapons, each one aimed to wound, each one striking a raw nerve. Tears streamed down Sira's face, a mixture of pain, fear, and exhaustion. Keith watched her, his own anger melting into remorse. He realized that his attempts at reassurance had been clumsy, inadequate, lacking the empathy and understanding she desperately needed. He'd dismissed her anxieties as drama, failing to recognize the depth of her fear and insecurity. He'd allowed his own self-doubt and anxieties to build a wall between them.

The argument reached a fever pitch, a chaotic exchange of accusations and recriminations. The carefully constructed façade of their relationship crumbled, revealing the raw nerves and deep-seated insecurities that threatened to tear them apart. Their voices rose, punctuated by sharp intakes of breath and the occasional sob. The vibrant hope that had once filled their home was now overshadowed by a heavy cloud of resentment and misunderstanding.

The silence that followed was even more deafening than the shouting. Sira sat on the sofa, her body trembling, her face buried in her hands. Keith stood near the window, the city lights blurring before his eyes. The weight of his actions, his failure to truly understand her, pressed down on him. He saw the depth of her pain, the vulnerability that he'd so carelessly ignored. He realized he hadn't been present, truly present, in their relationship. He'd been consumed by his own anxieties, blind to her struggles. He'd been so caught up in proving his worth that he'd forgotten to simply be there for her.

Hours later, the argument's echoes still lingered in the air. The exhaustion, both physical and emotional, hung heavy, a palpable barrier between them. Sira stared at the wall, replaying the hurtful things that had been said, the accusations that had cut so deeply. Keith, finally able to acknowledge the depth of his mistakes, approached her hesitantly. He sat beside her, his hand reaching out to gently touch her arm.

He didn't attempt to justify his actions; he didn't offer empty platitudes. He simply said, "I'm sorry, Sira. I was wrong. I messed up badly." His voice was raw with emotion, sincere and devoid of any defensiveness. He understood the depth of her hurt, the validity of her fears, and the way his actions had contributed to her emotional distress. He recognized that his actions had been rooted in his own insecurities, in his own anxieties about proving his worth.

Sira looked at him, her eyes still red-rimmed but softened by a glimmer of hope. She didn't immediately forgive him, but she saw the genuine remorse in his eyes, the sincere effort to understand and atone. He wasn't just offering an apology; he was offering a commitment to change, a promise to be present, to listen, to support her.

The road to reconciliation would be long and arduous. It would require honest introspection, open communication, and a willingness to confront their deepest insecurities and unresolved issues. But in the quiet aftermath of the storm, a fragile sense of hope emerged. In that quiet space, amidst the wreckage of their argument, a foundation for a stronger, more resilient relationship began to take shape. A foundation built not on the security of a house, but on the foundation of understanding, empathy, and the steadfast promise to be truly present for each other. The argument, though devastating, had become a catalyst, a turning point that pushed them towards a deeper understanding, a more mature and compassionate love.

An Apology with Understanding

The silence in the aftermath of their fight hung heavy, thick with unspoken words and simmering resentment. The house, once a symbol of their burgeoning future, felt suffocating, each room a stark reminder of their fractured relationship. Sira sat on the worn couch, her hands resting on her swollen belly, a silent sentinel guarding the life growing within. The exhaustion was bone-deep, a weariness that went beyond the physical demands of pregnancy. It was the exhaustion of carrying the weight of their unspoken anxieties, the pressure of navigating a relationship teetering on the brink.

Keith paced, the floorboards creaking under his restless feet. He hadn't intended to hurt Sira; he'd genuinely believed his late nights were harmless, a necessary escape from the mounting pressures of providing for them. But seeing the pain etched on Sira's face, the vulnerability in her usually bright eyes, a cold dread had settled in his gut. He hadn't considered the impact of his actions on her, consumed as he was by his own anxieties about finances and the unexpected responsibilities of adulthood. He realized, with a sickening lurch, that he had been selfish. He'd prioritized his own need for space and camaraderie over her need for reassurance and emotional support.

He stopped pacing and sank onto the floor, the plush carpet cushioning his fall. He watched Sira, the gentle rise and fall of her chest the only visible sign of life in the suffocating silence. The thought of losing her, of losing the child they were expecting, filled him with a terror he had never known before. His casual dismissals of her concerns now felt monstrous, unforgivable acts of emotional negligence.

He reached out a tentative hand, his fingers brushing against her arm. The slight tremor in his hand mirrored the turmoil in his heart. Sira didn't flinch, didn't pull away. The small gesture, a bridge across the chasm of their argument, was a silent invitation to begin the long process of healing.

"Sira," he began, his voice thick with emotion. The words caught in his throat, the weight of his apology pressing down on him. "I'm so incredibly sorry. I was wrong. I was a complete idiot."

He took a deep breath, needing the strength to articulate the depth of his regret. "I didn't see it, not really. I was so caught up in… in everything – the house, the money, my friends – that I didn't see how much it was hurting you. I didn't realize how insecure you felt, how alone you must have felt carrying this… this burden." He gestured towards her belly. "I should have been there for you, every step of the way. And I wasn't."

He confessed his initial misinterpretations of her anxieties, how he'd seen her concerns as a manipulative tactic rather than a genuine expression of fear and vulnerability. He spoke of his own insecurities, his fear of losing his friends, his fear of failure, his fear of not being good enough. He hadn't processed his own emotions effectively, and his flawed attempts to manage them had only served to push Sira further away. He admitted his childish need for reassurance from his ex-girlfriends, mistaking their friendship for a sign that his current relationship wasn't strong enough.

He didn't offer excuses, just honest admissions of his mistakes, his flaws. He spoke of his realization that his actions weren't just about him; they had real consequences for Sira and their relationship. The house, meant to be a haven, had become a source of contention. His late nights, intended to de-stress, had deepened the chasm between them. His attempts at emotional distance had instead fostered a sense of emotional isolation for Sira, fueling her fears and insecurities.

Sira listened, her gaze fixed on his face, her expression a mixture of hurt, skepticism, and cautious hope. Tears welled in her eyes, but they didn't fall. She needed to hear his words, to gauge the authenticity of his remorse. His honesty, the raw vulnerability in his voice, slowly chipped away at her defenses.

"It wasn't just about your friends, Keith," she said, her voice soft, her words carefully chosen. "It was about… feeling unseen, unheard. Like everything was a competition, a balancing act between them and me. And you always seemed to choose them, even when I was hurting."

Keith nodded, understanding dawning on his face. He had been so focused on his own needs and his own anxieties, he hadn't seen her pain. He hadn't understood that her insecurities weren't about him needing space from his friends, but about her fear of losing him, about her need for emotional security during a tumultuous period in their lives.

"I know," he said, his voice cracking slightly. "And I understand now. I understand what I did, and how much it hurt you. And I'm going to do everything in my power to make it right."

The conversation stretched on, a slow, painful unpacking of their emotions, their fears, their insecurities. Keith listened intently, absorbing every word, offering apologies and reassurances where necessary. He didn't try to minimize her feelings or dismiss her concerns. He listened, he validated, he acknowledged.

He shared his own anxieties about fatherhood, the fear of not being a good enough father, the pressure to provide and protect. He spoke of his regret for pushing her away, for failing to recognize and appreciate the immense strength and courage she was displaying. He spoke of the way his need for reassurance from his friends manifested as an avoidance of his anxieties about his relationship with Sira.

He vowed to change, to be more present, more attentive, more supportive. He talked about attending couples therapy, not just to mend their relationship but to better understand his own emotional patterns and learn healthier coping mechanisms. He committed to spending less time with his friends, not to exclude them entirely, but to prioritize Sira and the child they were expecting. He would learn to communicate his feelings effectively instead of retreating into silence or seeking external validation.

Sira, initially hesitant, gradually softened. His genuine remorse, his willingness to acknowledge his flaws, and his commitment to change began to melt her defenses. The weight on her shoulders seemed lighter, the fear and insecurity easing as she saw a glimmer of the man she loved emerging from beneath the layers of self-absorption and anxiety.

The conversation didn't erase the hurt, the pain of the past arguments. But it laid the foundation for a future built on understanding, empathy, and a genuine commitment to each other. It was a long and arduous road ahead, a journey that required constant effort, honest communication, and mutual forgiveness. But for the first time in a long time, Sira felt a flicker of hope. The house, though still a symbol of their anxieties, now felt like it had the potential to become a true home, a sanctuary of love and support, not just a physical space, but a representation of the stronger, more compassionate relationship they were building, brick by painful brick. The silence that followed was no longer heavy with resentment, but filled with the quiet promise of healing and growth. The love they shared, tested and battered, was not broken, but stronger, forged in the crucible of their confrontations and compromises.

Forgiveness and Acceptance

The next morning, sunlight streamed through the gaps in the curtains, painting stripes across the bedroom floor. Sira woke slowly, the weight of her anxieties momentarily lifted. The quiet hum of the refrigerator was the only sound, a stark contrast to the tempestuous night before. She turned to Keith, his arm draped across her waist, his breathing even and deep. He looked peaceful, utterly unaware of the turmoil that had raged within her just hours ago. A wave of tenderness washed over her, a potent antidote to the lingering bitterness.

She traced the line of his jaw, her fingers lingering on the stubble that had sprouted overnight. The Keith she saw now, the one asleep beside her, wasn't the man who had accused her of manipulation, the man whose words had pierced her heart like shards of glass. This Keith was vulnerable, exposed, his defenses down. And in his vulnerability, Sira found a space for her own forgiveness to bloom.

She sat up gently, careful not to disturb him, and went to the window. The world outside was bathed in a golden light, a new day dawning, full of possibilities. It was a day for fresh starts, a day to leave the past behind, to build something stronger and more resilient from the ashes of their argument.

Later, after Keith had woken, they sat at the kitchen table, the morning sun illuminating the space. The air between them was still charged, but the electricity was different now. It wasn't the crackling tension of conflict, but a subtle thrum of anticipation, a shared awareness of the delicate balance they were attempting to strike.

"I'm sorry," Keith said, his voice low and husky. "I was wrong. Completely wrong. I let my insecurities get the better of me. I didn't listen to you, and I didn't understand." He reached across the table, his hand covering hers. His touch was gentle, reassuring.

Sira squeezed his hand. "I understand," she replied, her voice thick with emotion. "I was scared, Keith. Terrified, actually. Becoming a mother is terrifying, and all the other things...the financial pressures, your exes…it's a lot to handle. And maybe I didn't express myself well, maybe I lashed out, but it wasn't to manipulate you." A tear escaped her eye, tracing a path down her cheek.

"I know," he whispered, his thumb gently wiping away the tear. "And I should have been there for you. I should have supported you, not made you feel like you were walking on eggshells." He paused, searching for the right words. "I've been thinking about everything you said last night, about how stressed you've been, about how much you're carrying."

They talked for a long time that morning, a conversation that flowed seamlessly between apologies and explanations, between shared vulnerabilities and promises for the future. Keith spoke of his own anxieties, his fear of losing her, his fear of not being a good father. He admitted to the lingering insecurities he felt about his ex-girlfriends, the fear that their friendship was a threat to their relationship. He confessed to the guilt he carried, the feeling that he had not given Sira the support she deserved.

Sira, in turn, shared her fears, her anxieties about the financial burden, her worries about being a good mother, and her need for reassurance. She acknowledged her own flaws, her tendency to overthink, to jump to conclusions. Most importantly, she expressed her love for him, a love that had been tested, but not broken. She explained how the weight of her pregnancy, compounded by her worries about his insecurities and his relationships with other women had pushed her to the edge. She explained how she had felt unheard and misunderstood.

Their conversation wasn't a magical erasure of the past, but a turning point. It was a testament to their commitment to work through their problems, a willingness to understand each other's perspectives, and to build a stronger foundation for their future together. The pain lingered, the scars remained, but they were no longer insurmountable barriers. They were reminders of the challenges they had faced, lessons learned, and a testament to the strength of their love.

The following weeks were a period of healing and rebuilding. They sought couples' therapy, a safe space where they could explore their unresolved issues in a guided environment. The therapist helped them to communicate more effectively, to identify their triggers, and to develop healthier coping mechanisms. They learned to express their needs and concerns without resorting to accusations or blame.

Keith made a conscious effort to address Sira's concerns, to be more present, more supportive, and more understanding. He started spending less time with his ex-girlfriends, not because he was cutting them out of his life, but because he wanted to prioritize his relationship with Sira, especially given her pregnancy and the emotional turmoil it caused her. He also actively participated in the preparations for their child's arrival, tackling chores and errands with a newfound diligence. He tried to understand the financial pressures they faced and helped to develop a more manageable budget.

Sira, in turn, learned to communicate her needs and anxieties more effectively, to articulate her fears without resorting to anger or resentment. She allowed Keith space to express his own feelings and insecurities without feeling threatened or judged. She understood that his anxieties, though rooted in his own experiences and insecurities, were real and deserved her empathy. She also actively engaged in self-care, recognizing the importance of prioritizing her mental and emotional well-being.

One evening, as they sat on the couch, Sira's head resting on Keith's shoulder, the house felt different. It no longer felt suffocating; instead, it hummed with a quiet sense of peace. The silence wasn't an absence of sound, but a comforting presence, a shared understanding built on trust and mutual respect. The feeling of impending parenthood wasn't as daunting; instead, it was accompanied by the comforting weight of their shared love and the promise of a future filled with joy, even if it also held the challenges and uncertainties inherent to parenthood and life in general.

The pregnancy itself took on a new dimension. It was no longer a source of contention, but a shared experience, a bond that deepened their connection. They spoke about baby names, planned the nursery, and dreamt about their child's future, their voices filled with hope and excitement. The anxieties still lingered, but they were now tempered by a sense of shared purpose, a mutual commitment to navigate the challenges of parenthood together. They had been tested, battered, almost broken; but they had come out stronger, their bond forged in the crucible of conflict and compromise, their love a testament to their unwavering commitment to each other.

The house, once a symbol of their anxieties and disagreements, had transformed into a home, a safe haven where their love could thrive and flourish, a foundation built upon understanding, forgiveness, and a shared promise to face the future, hand in hand. The journey was far from over, but for the first time, they felt truly ready, armed with the lessons learned and the strength of their renewed love. The unexpected visit from Sira's high school ex-boyfriend still loomed, a potential challenge awaiting them on their road ahead. However, the couple faced it, not with fear, but with confidence borne from their newfound ability to communicate effectively, to forgive, and to build their relationship brick by brick. The foundation had been laid, and now they were ready to face whatever storms lay ahead. The future, once shrouded in uncertainty, now held a promise of brighter days, a promise they were prepared to embrace together.

Addressing Financial Concerns

The quiet hum of the refrigerator, a constant companion in their new home, was a far cry from the tumultuous arguments of the previous night. Sira, sipping lukewarm coffee, watched Keith pace the kitchen, the early morning sunlight catching the worry lines etched around his eyes. The house, a symbol of their commitment, now felt heavy with the weight of their financial reality. Buying it had been a leap of faith, fueled by love and a desperate need for stability, but the initial euphoria had faded, replaced by the stark reality of mortgage payments, utility bills, and the looming cost of raising a child.

"We need a plan," Sira said softly, her voice breaking the silence. Keith stopped pacing, turning to her with a weary sigh. The exhaustion etched on his face mirrored her own. The sleepless nights weren't just fueled by anxieties about their relationship; they were also plagued by the constant pressure of money.

"I know," he replied, running a hand through his hair. "But where do we even begin?"

The conversation that followed was a mixture of apprehension and pragmatism. They laid out their finances on the kitchen table – Keith's salary from his software engineering job, Sira's part-time freelance writing income, which had dwindled since her pregnancy, and the small amount saved before the house purchase. The numbers were stark, revealing a deficit that loomed like a dark cloud.

"My freelance work… it's not consistent enough," Sira admitted, her voice barely above a whisper. "And with the baby coming, I won't be able to work as much."

Keith nodded, his expression grim. "We need to increase our income somehow. I could work overtime, but that'll eat into our time together." He paused, then added, "We could also consider renting out a room. It wouldn't be ideal, but it would help with the mortgage."

The idea of strangers living in their house felt intrusive, a violation of the intimacy they'd painstakingly built. But the alternative – struggling to make ends meet, constantly stressed, and potentially facing foreclosure – was even more daunting.

"We could explore that option," Sira conceded, her voice tight. "Maybe a trusted friend or family member? Someone we feel comfortable with."

Their brainstorming session extended throughout the day, a blend of practical solutions and emotional considerations. They investigated possibilities like selling some of their less essential belongings, cutting down on unnecessary expenses, and exploring cheaper insurance options. Every small decision felt monumental, weighed down by the significance of their precarious financial situation.

Keith, determined to solve the problem, spent hours researching ways to boost his income. He discovered online coding courses that could enhance his skills and potentially lead to higher-paying jobs. The thought of long nights studying, alongside the demands of his current job and their new life together, felt overwhelming. But the prospect of a more secure future for his family fueled his determination.

He looked at Sira, his expression softening. "I'll do this, for us."

Sira, seeing the determination in his eyes, felt a surge of love and gratitude. She knew that this wouldn't be easy; it would demand sacrifices from both of them. But the shared commitment to overcome this challenge strengthened their bond, forging a resilience that transcended their financial worries.

Their discussions weren't always easy. They argued, sometimes fiercely, about priorities and sacrifices. There were moments of doubt, of fear that their dreams were slipping away. But through it all, their love served as a constant anchor, pulling them back from the brink of despair.

They decided to create a detailed budget, a daunting task that forced them to confront their spending habits. Tracking every expense, from groceries to entertainment, brought a sobering realization of how much they were spending on non-essential items. They agreed to cut back on dining out, opting for home-cooked meals. They cancelled their expensive streaming subscriptions, opting for free alternatives. Every small cutback felt like a victory, a step closer to financial stability.

The prospect of renting out a room remained a sensitive topic. They decided to explore the possibility of renting out the guest room, but only to someone they knew and trusted. They reached out to Sira's cousin, Vina, who was struggling to find affordable housing. She was overjoyed at the prospect and readily agreed. Having a trusted family member as a housemate eased their anxieties significantly.

Beyond the immediate financial issues, they also addressed the underlying causes of their financial stress. Sira, acknowledging her anxieties about their relationship, sought further support from her therapist. She confessed her insecurities about their financial situation and its potential impact on their relationship. Through therapy, she learned to manage her anxieties, communicating her concerns openly with Keith without resorting to accusations or blame. This improved communication allowed them to work together effectively, understanding each other's perspectives and challenges.

The process of addressing their financial concerns wasn't a quick fix, but a journey of growth and resilience. It required compromise, communication, and an unwavering commitment to their future together. The shared struggle, however challenging, ultimately strengthened their bond. Their newfound financial prudence, though born out of necessity, cultivated a greater appreciation for the things that truly mattered. It was a hard-won lesson, etched into the foundation of their relationship and their new home. The house, once a source of tension and stress, now felt like a sanctuary—a testament to their perseverance, their love, and their ability to face challenges head-on, together. The weight of their financial worries hadn't completely vanished; it had simply transformed into a shared burden, a challenge they were tackling side-by-side, their love solidifying with every obstacle overcome. The journey ahead was still uncertain, but for the first time, they felt truly prepared, equipped not only with a plan, but with a renewed sense of partnership and a steadfast belief in their shared future. The looming arrival of their baby brought a new dimension to their commitment, a sense of responsibility that further cemented their determination to overcome their challenges and build a secure and loving future for their family. The unexpected visit from Sira's high school ex-boyfriend was still looming on the horizon, but the newly-forged strength in their relationship gave them the confidence to face it, to navigate any potential storm with a sense of unity and resolve that had previously been absent. They had weathered a financial tempest; they were ready to face whatever came next. The future, once a blurry, anxious landscape, had begun to resolve itself into a clearer, more hopeful picture, one painted with the enduring colors of their love and the strength of their newfound financial resilience.

Strengthening Communication

The therapist's advice echoed in Sira's mind: "Honest, open communication is the cornerstone of any strong relationship." It was easier said than done, especially when emotions ran high, as they had been lately. The financial strain, the looming arrival of their baby, and the lingering shadows of Keith's past relationships had created a chasm between them, a silent gulf that seemed impossible to bridge. But Sira was determined to try.

That evening, after everything had settled down, Sira down next to Keith, she gently touched his arm. He looked up from his phone, his expression guarded. "Keith," she began, her voice soft, "I want to talk about us."

Keith hesitated, then nodded, setting his phone down. He pulled her close, his touch hesitant, as if unsure of how to navigate this delicate terrain. "Okay," he said, his voice a low murmur. "What's on your mind?"

Sira took a deep breath, gathering her thoughts. "I know we've been fighting a lot lately," she admitted. "And I know a lot of it stems from my insecurities. Seeing your exes around, worrying about money… it all gets to me."

Keith's eyes softened. "I understand," he said, his voice filled with a sincerity that reassured her. "I haven't been great at handling things either. I should have been more sensitive to your feelings, more understanding."

This was a start, Sira thought. A genuine acknowledgement of their failings, a shared responsibility for the strain on their relationship. "It's not just about your exes," she continued. "It's about us. About learning to communicate better. About really listening to each other, without getting defensive."

"I agree," Keith replied. "I feel like we've been talking past each other, not to each other. I get so caught up in my own worries that I don't focus on how you're feeling."

They spent the next hour talking, really talking. Sira confessed her anxieties about motherhood, her fear of not being a good enough mother, her concerns about the financial burdens that lay ahead. Keith listened, not interrupting, offering words of comfort and reassurance. He shared his own insecurities, his fear of failing as a father, his worries about providing for his family.

It wasn't a perfect conversation. There were still moments of tension, fleeting glimpses of the old patterns they were trying to break. But the overall tone was different. It was a conversation built on honesty, vulnerability, and a mutual desire to understand each other.

One of the key changes was their active listening. Before, when they argued, it often devolved into a shouting match, each trying to talk over the other, their voices fueled by frustration and hurt. Now, they focused on truly hearing what the other was saying. They asked clarifying questions, offering empathetic responses rather than immediate defensiveness. They practiced mirroring each other's feelings to show understanding, a technique their therapist had suggested.

"I understand you're feeling overwhelmed by the financial pressure," Keith would say, mirroring Sira's feelings, before offering a solution or expressing his own understanding. This simple act of acknowledging her emotions first, before offering a solution, created a safe space for her to express herself fully, without fear of interruption or dismissal.

Sira, in turn, practiced active listening when Keith voiced his concerns about his friends and exes. Instead of jumping to conclusions or getting defensive, she would pause, and ask clarifying questions, giving him space to express himself without interruption. This created an atmosphere of mutual respect and understanding, helping to heal the wounds caused by misunderstandings.

They also implemented a new system of communication, a "check-in" time each evening before bed. This wasn't a formal, scheduled meeting, but rather a dedicated time for them to reconnect, to share their day, their worries, their hopes. It was a chance to debrief, to process their emotions, and to reinforce their bond.

The change wasn't immediate. There were still bumps in the road, moments of frustration, times when old habits resurfaced. But the effort was there, a conscious commitment to building a stronger foundation for their relationship. They practiced empathy, patience, and understanding. They learned to express their needs clearly and respectfully, avoiding accusatory language. They focused on finding solutions together, rather than assigning blame.

One evening, while discussing the upcoming baby shower, a disagreement arose regarding the guest list. Previously, this would have led to a heated argument. But this time, Sira took a deep breath. "Keith," she said calmly, "I understand you want to invite everyone, but I'm feeling a bit overwhelmed by the thought of a large gathering. Maybe we can compromise and keep it smaller, just close family and friends?"

Keith listened, really listened. He saw the stress in her eyes, the exhaustion etched on her face. "Okay," he said softly. "We can do it your way. I want you to be comfortable."

This was a pivotal moment. A simple compromise, but one that demonstrated a fundamental shift in their communication. It wasn't about winning or losing; it was about finding common ground, about prioritizing each other's well-being.

The improved communication wasn't just confined to their personal struggles. It extended to their financial concerns. They started budgeting together, transparently discussing their expenses and income. They made joint decisions, pooling their resources, and collaborating on financial goals. This shared responsibility fostered a sense of partnership, turning their financial challenges into a shared journey, a testament to their growing trust and understanding.

As the weeks passed, the changes became more noticeable. Their arguments became less frequent, their conversations more meaningful. The house, once a source of tension, now felt like a sanctuary, filled with the warmth of their renewed connection. The love they shared wasn't just a feeling; it was a conscious choice, a commitment they reinforced every day through their improved communication. The arrival of their baby brought a new level of intimacy and shared responsibility, further cementing their bond. They were no longer just a couple; they were a team, a family, bound together not just by love, but by a shared commitment to understanding, communication, and unwavering support.

The arrival of Sira's high school ex-boyfriend was met not with panic and suspicion, but with a calm resolve. They faced the situation together, discussing their concerns and anxieties openly and honestly. The experience, while challenging, only strengthened their bond further, proving the resilience of their improved communication and the depth of their commitment to each other. Their journey had been difficult, filled with challenges that threatened to tear them apart. But through it all, their unwavering commitment to strengthening their communication had been their guiding light, a beacon illuminating their path toward a stronger, more fulfilling future together.

Chapter 4:

Ex, High School

The bell above the door of "The Daily Grind" jingled, announcing a new customer. Sira, momentarily distracted from meticulously arranging pastries on the display counter, glanced up. Her breath hitched. Standing awkwardly near the entrance, clutching a slightly crumpled paper coffee cup, was Noah. Noah. Her high school sweetheart, the boy who had held her hand through countless awkward dances and tearful breakups, the boy she'd thought she'd forgotten.

He hadn't changed much. Still the same unruly brown hair, the same hesitant smile that could melt glaciers. But the boyish charm was tempered with a hint of maturity, a suggestion of the man he'd become in the intervening years. He looked… different. Older, sure, but also… sharper. His eyes, the same warm brown she remembered, held a depth she hadn't noticed back then.

"Sira?" he said, his voice a soft murmur that still held the familiar lilt.

The blood rushed to her cheeks. Her carefully constructed composure crumbled. This was not how she envisioned her Tuesday afternoon. Not with a mountain of paperwork awaiting her at the apartment, not with the constant gnawing anxiety of her pregnancy and her strained relationship with Keith. And definitely not with Noah, her past, suddenly materializing in the most inconvenient of places.

"Noah?" she replied, her voice barely a whisper. The other customers seemed oblivious to the mini-earthquake rumbling through her internal landscape.

He shuffled forward, a hesitant smile playing on his lips. "Wow, you haven't changed a bit," he said, his eyes lingering on her for a moment longer than polite conversation demanded. The compliment, while genuine, felt awkward, charged with unspoken history.

Sira managed a weak smile. "You haven't either," she replied, her mind desperately searching for a graceful exit strategy. This wasn't just a casual encounter; it was a ghost from a past life, a past she'd carefully tucked away, believing it safely buried beneath the complexities of her current reality.

He chuckled, a low rumble in his chest that resonated with a surprising amount of confidence. "Except maybe taller?" he added, his eyes twinkling. The lightness in his tone was a stark contrast to the turmoil churning within her.

"A little," she admitted, acutely aware of the bump beneath her apron. The subtle reminder of her pregnancy added another layer of complexity to this already charged reunion.

"I… I saw your picture on Keith's Facebook page," he said, his voice softening. "Congratulations." He spoke the word "Keith" with a neutral tone, masking any potential jealousy or resentment. At least, she hoped it was masked.

The mention of Keith, her current partner, the man who was the father of her unborn child, the man who was currently grappling with a crisis of confidence stemming from her pregnancy and the lingering presence of his own ex-girlfriends, sent another wave of anxiety through Sira.

She felt a prickle of guilt, a familiar pang of insecurity. Why was Noah here? What did he want? And more importantly, how would Keith react to this unexpected encounter?

"Thanks," she murmured, trying to keep her voice steady. She focused on the rhythmic clinking of the coffee machine in the background, a small anchor in the rising tide of her emotions. "It's… been a while." An understatement, she thought. It had been years, years filled with growth, heartache, and significant life changes.

He nodded, pushing a stray lock of hair from his forehead, a gesture that felt both familiar and strangely alien. "Yeah, it has. I… I'm in town for a few days, visiting family. I saw your name on a bakery sign and… well, I thought I'd say hi."

His explanation felt genuine, lacking any undercurrent of malice or romantic pursuit. Still, a knot of apprehension tightened in her stomach. The ease with which he'd re-entered her life, the casualness of his explanation, unsettled her. She wondered if he realized the implications of his presence, the precarious balance he was potentially disrupting.

"That's… nice," she stammered, acutely aware of the inadequacy of her response. The word seemed to hang in the air, a pathetic attempt to bridge the chasm of years and untold experiences.

He seemed to sense her discomfort, his smile faltering slightly. "Look, I don't want to intrude," he said, his voice laced with a hint of regret. "But… it's good to see you."

"It's good to see you too," Sira replied, her voice a little stronger this time. She wondered if this encounter was a coincidence, a random act of fate, or a calculated move. She knew she wouldn't find out without a conversation.

He hesitated for a moment, then took a step back. "Well," he said, "I should get going. Enjoy your day."

"You too," Sira replied, watching him walk away, a mix of relief and curiosity swirling within her. The bell above the door jingled again, this time marking his departure and leaving Sira alone with the lingering scent of coffee and the overwhelming weight of her complicated life. She had a feeling this was far from over. The unexpected appearance of Noah wasn't just a fleeting moment; it was a new chapter in her life, a chapter filled with uncertainty, but also the potential for unforeseen complications. And she knew, deep down, that this reunion wouldn't be easily resolved. It wouldn't be simple; it wouldn't be clean. It was another challenge, another obstacle in her already complicated relationship with Keith.

The weight of her situation pressed down on her, the pregnancy, Keith's insecurities, and now, Noah. She needed to tell Keith. But the thought of his reaction sent a shiver down her spine. Jealousy, anger, confusion – all of these emotions were potential outcomes. And the uncertainty was almost unbearable. She needed to figure out how to navigate this new, unpredictable situation, how to navigate the delicate balance of her present and the ghost of her past. She sighed, the aroma of pastries suddenly unappealing. Her day, it seemed, had just become significantly more complicated.

The rest of her shift passed in a blur of activity. She mechanically served customers, their cheerful chatter a stark contrast to the storm brewing inside her. The image of

Noah's hesitant smile, the warmth in his eyes, kept flashing before her eyes, a stark contrast to the often tense interactions she'd been having with Keith lately. The anxieties she'd been feeling regarding their relationship, and the impending arrival of their child, felt magnified a hundred times.

As soon as she finished her shift, she rushed home, the familiar weight of her pregnancy heavier than usual. Keith was already there, engrossed in a video game, oblivious to the turmoil raging within her. The comfortable silence of their apartment, usually a source of comfort, felt oppressive, suffocating.

"Keith," she began, her voice barely audible above the sounds of the game.

He glanced up, his brow furrowed in momentary confusion. "Hey," he replied, his attention still partially on the screen. His disinterest wasn't deliberate cruelty, just the automatic response of someone deeply immersed in a digital world.

"I need to talk to you," Sira said, her voice gaining strength. She needed to tell him. The longer she waited, the worse it would become. She owed him the truth, and herself the relief of sharing her burden.

He paused the game, his eyes finally meeting hers. The sudden shift in his demeanor was noticeable. A flicker of concern crossed his face, quickly replaced by his usual guardedness. "What is it?" he asked, his voice laced with a hint of apprehension.

Sira took a deep breath, stealing herself for his reaction. She recounted her encounter with Noah, carefully choosing her words, trying to minimize the emotional drama. She described his appearance, his casual conversation, the reasons he gave for being in town. She left out the details that could inflame his insecurities, focusing on the factual aspects of their encounter. As she spoke, she watched him, searching his face for any indication of jealousy, any sign of the insecurities that had been plaguing their relationship.

He listened intently, his expression unreadable. When she finished, he remained silent for a long moment, his eyes fixed on a distant point, his mind clearly racing. Sira's heart pounded in her chest, the silence between them filled with unspoken anxieties. She desperately wished she could understand his inner thoughts, decode the emotions concealed behind the mask of composure.

Finally, he spoke. "So… he's just… visiting?" he asked, his voice low, almost a whisper. His words were neutral, but the tremor in his voice gave him away, betraying the hidden currents of insecurity and jealousy within.

"Yes," Sira replied, her own voice wavering. She reached out and gently touched his hand, a silent plea for understanding, for empathy.

He looked down at their joined hands, then back up at her face. The tension in his body was palpable. "Okay," he finally said, his voice still low but firmer this time. "Okay. I understand."

The "Okay" didn't fully convey his feelings. It was a shield erected against the vulnerabilities threatening to overwhelm him. Sira knew it. She sensed the unease, the unspoken questions lingering beneath his calm exterior.

"It's just… a lot," she said softly, her voice thick with emotion. The pregnancy, the financial strain, her anxieties, Keith's insecurities, and now Noah. The weight of it all was almost unbearable.

He nodded, a flicker of understanding in his eyes. He pulled her closer, enveloping her in a hug, the warmth of his body a small comfort amid the storm. For the moment, the tension eased, replaced by a fragile sense of unity. But the appearance of Noah had undeniably shaken the foundation of their relationship, exposing its fragility, its susceptibility to external pressures. They still had a long way to go, many challenges to overcome. The road ahead wouldn't be easy, and the path towards a stable, loving future would require continuous effort, patience, and unwavering commitment. But as they held each other, for a moment, a shared sense of hope flickered between them. This was just another test, another obstacle on their journey. And they would face it, together.

Emotional Storm

The hug from Noah, a fleeting comfort, left Sira trembling. It wasn't the hug itself, but the tidal wave of memories it unleashed. The scent of his cologne, a familiar blend of sandalwood and something subtly citrusy, triggered a cascade of images: stolen kisses under the bleachers, whispered secrets during late-night study sessions, the bittersweet ache of their first heartbreak. These memories, carefully tucked away in the recesses of her mind, now swarmed, vivid and unsettling. She felt a disorienting blend of nostalgia and guilt, a potent cocktail that left her nauseous.

Pulling away, she saw the uncertainty etched on Noah's face, mirroring her own turmoil. He looked different, older, the boyish charm replaced with a hint of weariness around the eyes. But beneath the surface, she recognized him – the Noah who made her laugh until her sides hurt, the Noah who understood her in a way no one else ever had.

The initial shock gave way to a deeper, more insidious unease. The sight of Noah wasn't just a nostalgic trip down memory lane; it was a stark reminder of the life she almost lived, the life she had consciously chosen to leave behind. This life with Keith, chaotic and demanding as it was, was her reality. It was a reality filled with financial anxieties, the ever-present shadow of Keith's ex-girlfriends, and now, the overwhelming responsibility of carrying their child. Yet, Noah's presence had cracked open the veil of her contentment, exposing the vulnerabilities she had worked so hard to conceal.

The pastry shop, usually her sanctuary, felt suffocating. The sweet aroma of freshly baked bread, usually a source of comfort, now felt cloying, almost suffocating. She longed to escape, to run, to find some quiet corner where she could unravel the tangled threads of her emotions without judgment. But Noah was still there, his gaze holding hers, silently acknowledging the storm raging within her.

"Sira...," he began, his voice hesitant, a stark contrast to the confident, playful tone she remembered. "I... I didn't mean to..."

His words were lost in the whirlwind of her thoughts. The image of Keith, his face etched with concern, flashed in her mind. She pictured his hand on her stomach, the tender way he spoke to their unborn child. The guilt intensified, a heavy cloak weighing down her already burdened spirit. What would Keith think? How would he react? The thought was a sharp, stabbing pain.

Noah's presence was a catalyst, bringing to the surface a fear she hadn't fully acknowledged: the fear that she wasn't truly happy with Keith, that a part of her still yearned for the simplicity, the uncomplicated love of her past. The thought terrified her. She had invested so much in this relationship, in this life with Keith. The house, the impending birth of their child – these were tangible symbols of her commitment, and the idea of abandoning it all was both liberating and terrifying.

She managed a weak smile, a fragile mask concealing the turmoil within. "It's okay, Noah," she whispered, her voice barely audible above the hum of the coffee machine. "It's… it's good to see you."

The lie hung heavy in the air, suffocating her with its insincerity. It was good to see him, in a way. But it was also unsettling, a jarring reminder of the choices she had made, and the uncertainties that still lingered in her heart. The conversation that followed was stilted, awkward, a dance around unspoken feelings and unspoken truths. They spoke of inconsequential things – the weather, their respective jobs, their families. But beneath the surface current of polite conversation, a deeper current flowed, a silent acknowledgment of a shared history, a connection that time and distance couldn't completely erase.

Later, after Noah had left, the full weight of her emotional exhaustion crashed down on Sira. She leaned against the counter, the cool ceramic a small comfort against the burning heat of her cheeks. She replayed their encounter in her head, dissecting every word, every gesture, searching for clues, for answers she knew she might not find. The fear of losing Keith, the fear of betraying him, the fear of being overwhelmed by the complexities of her life – these emotions were a suffocating blanket, smothering her with their weight.

She had convinced herself that her anxieties stemmed from Keith's inability to fully comprehend her emotional struggles, his perceived lack of support in dealing with his ex-girlfriends. But the meeting with Noah exposed a deeper, more personal insecurity: the uncertainty about her own feelings. Had she truly moved on from Noah? Or had she merely buried her feelings, pushing them deep down where they festered, waiting for an opportunity to resurface?

The thought of telling Keith about Noah felt like a betrayal, a confession that could shatter the already fragile foundations of their relationship. She imagined his reaction: the hurt, the confusion, the anger. The image of his face contorted in pain was enough to make her stomach churn.

That night, curled up in the familiar comfort of their bed, the emptiness gnawed at her. She felt a profound sense of loneliness, a void that even Keith's presence couldn't completely fill. She couldn't sleep, the events of the day replaying themselves in her mind, a relentless loop of guilt and self-doubt. The anticipation of motherhood, once a source of joy, now felt like an added weight, a responsibility she wasn't sure she could bear alone.

The following days were a blur of anxiety and avoidance. She avoided Keith, consumed by a desire to process her feelings before facing him. The idea of confronting him with the possibility that she was still harboring feelings for her ex was almost unbearable. She knew that Keith had his own vulnerabilities, his own insecurities. His possessiveness stemmed from a deep-seated fear of losing her, a fear that was now exacerbated by her pregnancy and the looming challenges ahead.

Sira found herself gravitating towards her therapist's office, the comfortable setting, a welcome escape from the turmoil of her life. The therapist listened patiently, offering guidance and support. She helped Sira untangle the complex web of her emotions, acknowledging the validity of her feelings while encouraging her to find a path towards self-acceptance and reconciliation.

The therapist encouraged Sira to make a journal, a practice she initially resisted. But as she began to pour her thoughts and emotions onto paper, she began to see a pattern, a recurring theme of self-doubt and a fear of commitment. She realized that her anxiety wasn't solely about Keith's ex-girlfriends or his initial reluctance to fully grasp the depth of her anxieties during her pregnancy; it was a deeper, more ingrained fear of vulnerability and intimacy. Noah's reappearance had brought these unresolved issues to the forefront, forcing her to confront them.

The therapist suggested that Sira's anxieties might stem from a fear of repeating past mistakes. Her relationship with Noah, though idyllic in memory, had ultimately ended, leaving scars that lingered even years later. This fear, subconsciously amplified by the complexities of her current relationship with Keith, contributed to her insecurity and emotional turmoil.

As Sira continued to journal and attend therapy sessions, she gradually started to gain a clearer perspective on her feelings. She realized that while she had shared a special bond with Noah, their past was exactly that – the past. Her present relationship with Keith, despite its challenges, was built on a foundation of mutual respect and commitment. The imperfections, the anxieties, the insecurities – these were all part of the journey, the messy, unpredictable path of love and growth.

Through therapy, Sira also began to understand that her anxieties weren't solely her burden to bear. She realized that Keith needed to be involved in this process. He needed to understand the depth of her emotional struggles, not just the surface manifestations. It was time for an honest conversation, a conversation filled with vulnerability and a shared commitment to work through their issues together.

The path ahead would still be challenging, but with open communication and mutual understanding, she believed they could navigate the complexities of their relationship and emerge stronger, more resilient, and ultimately, happier. The unexpected reunion with Noah, though initially a source of distress, had become an unexpected spark for personal growth and a deeper understanding of her own emotional landscape. It was a turning point, a step towards a more mature and honest relationship with both herself and Keith.

Reaction and Jealousy

The car ride home was tense, a suffocating silence punctuated only by the rhythmic thump of the tires on the highway. Sira stared out the window, the blurring landscape mirroring the turmoil in her mind. Noah's unexpected appearance had stirred something within her, a flicker of a past she thought she'd long buried. It wasn't a passionate rekindling, not exactly, but a gentle stirring of memories, a wistful longing for a simpler time. She'd felt a pang of guilt, a momentary lapse in her complete devotion to Keith, and the knowledge of this unsettled her.

Keith, however, remained silent, his jaw clenched, his knuckles white as he gripped the steering wheel. His silence was far more unsettling than any outburst. He was usually so expressive, his emotions painted across his face like a vibrant masterpiece. This controlled quiet was a storm brewing beneath the surface, a tempest of unspoken resentment and jealousy.

Finally, as they pulled into the driveway of their new home – a house that represented a monumental leap of faith and a significant investment on Keith's part – he spoke, his voice low and strained. "Who was that?"

Sira flinched. She'd hoped he hadn't noticed the way her eyes had lingered on Noah, the way her smile had stretched a little too wide, a little too long. "It was Noah," she replied, her voice barely a whisper. "From high school."

The silence descended again, heavier this time, thicker with unspoken accusations. Keith turned to her, his gaze intense, searching. "And?" he prompted, the single word hanging in the air like a lead weight.

"And… we talked for a little while," Sira explained, trying to keep her voice steady, her heart pounding against her ribs. "He was just… passing through town. It was unexpected."

"Unexpected?" Keith echoed, his tone laced with skepticism. "He just happened to be in town, and he just happened to find you?"

Sira sighed, the tension in the car becoming almost palpable. "Yes, Keith. It was a coincidence."

He didn't respond immediately, his eyes fixed on hers, searching for any hint of deception. The silence stretched, filled with unspoken anxieties and simmering resentment. It was a silence that felt heavier than the pregnant pause before a storm. The air crackled with unspoken words, unacknowledged feelings.

"He... hugged you," Keith finally said, the words barely audible, a mere breath against the silence. It wasn't a question, but a statement, heavy with accusation. He wasn't asking for confirmation; he was merely acknowledging the visible truth.

Sira nodded, her throat constricting. The hug had been innocent enough, a brief moment of connection between two people from a shared past. Yet, in Keith's eyes, it seemed to have taken on a life of its own, a betrayal of their current relationship. She could almost feel his jealousy wrapping around her like a venomous vine, constricting her, suffocating her.

"It was just a friendly hug," she clarified, attempting to diffuse the tension, her voice wavering slightly. "We haven't seen each other in years."

"Years," he repeated, the word dripping with sarcasm. The bitterness in his tone was a stark contrast to the usually warm, loving man she knew. The jealousy was almost suffocating, its tendrils wrapping around her, constricting her breathing.

She tried to explain, to articulate the complexities of the emotions swirling within her, but the words caught in her throat. The memories of Noah, though bittersweet, were not a betrayal. They were simply a part of her past, a chapter that had closed long ago. But Keith's reaction made her question everything, made her doubt the strength of their relationship, the foundation of their life together.

Keith's jealousy wasn't new. It had been a simmering undercurrent in their relationship for months, fueled by his insecurity and Sira's past relationships. The fact that he was still friendly with his ex-girlfriends had never bothered Sira to the extent that this unexpected encounter with Noah had. It had always been a point of contention, a source of friction between them. He'd often accuse her of wanting to distance him from his friends, of wanting to control his life, of using the pregnancy as a means of isolating him.

His reaction to Noah felt different, more primal, more intense. It was as if the appearance of her ex-boyfriend had triggered something deep within him, a raw, visceral fear of losing her, of losing the life they had painstakingly built together.

The drive to their house, usually a comfortable journey punctuated by laughter and shared jokes, was now a silent, agonizing trek across a landscape of unspoken accusations and simmering resentment. The silence hung heavy in the air, a suffocating blanket woven from unspoken fears and insecurities.

Once inside, Keith stalked to the sofa, slumping onto it with a defeated sigh. The usually vibrant colors of their living room seemed dull and muted, reflecting the oppressive mood that had settled over them. Sira watched him, a mixture of sadness and frustration welling up inside her. She wished she could make him understand, make him see that her emotions were complex, that a hug didn't equate to a betrayal, that her past didn't negate her present.

"Keith," she began, approaching him cautiously, her voice soft, "Can we talk?"

He didn't respond, his gaze fixed on some unseen point on the floor, his shoulders slumped in dejection. He seemed to be wrestling with his own thoughts, battling internal demons that Sira couldn't reach.

Sira sat beside him, placing a hand gently on his arm. His muscles were tense, rigid under her touch. He didn't pull away, didn't react in any way. It was the stillness of his body, the lack of any outward expression, that felt the most painful.

"I understand you're upset," she said softly, choosing her words carefully, trying to find the right balance between empathy and assertion. "But Noah was just a memory, a fleeting moment from a different time. It doesn't change how I feel about you. It doesn't change anything between us."

He finally looked at her, his eyes filled with a mixture of pain and confusion. He looked weary, worn down by his own insecurities and anxieties. The Keith she loved, the man who had made her laugh until her sides ached, the man who had proposed amidst a field of sunflowers, seemed distant, lost in the fog of his own making.

"It's not just about Noah," he finally confessed, his voice barely a whisper. "It's about everything. The pregnancy, the financial pressure, the constant stress… I'm scared, Sira. I'm scared of losing you, of losing everything we've built."

His confession surprised her. It was a vulnerability she hadn't seen in him before, a raw display of his fears. It was the fear of inadequacy, a fear of not being enough, a fear of losing her to life's uncertainties. He didn't just fear the loss of Sira, but the loss of their future together, the crumbling foundation of their carefully constructed life.

His words hit her like a wave, washing over her with the force of an emotional tsunami. She saw a man overwhelmed by life's burdens, a man struggling under the weight of his responsibilities, a man desperately afraid of failure. His jealousy, she realized, was merely a symptom of a deeper underlying fear—the fear of losing not just her, but the carefully constructed life they had built together.

The house, the financial stress, the pregnancy – all of it contributed to this overwhelming sense of insecurity. The unexpected arrival of Noah had simply served as a catalyst, a trigger that brought all his anxieties to the surface.

"I know," Sira said softly, taking his hand in hers, her touch gentle, reassuring. "And I'm here. We'll face these things together. We'll work through it. We'll find a way."

The conversation that followed was long and difficult, filled with tears, admissions, and promises. It was a conversation that stripped away the layers of pretense and exposed the raw vulnerability beneath. Sira, in her own way, understood the depth of Keith's insecurities. She saw the man behind the jealousy, the man burdened by expectations, the man desperately afraid of failure.

That night, as they lay in bed, the weight of the day still heavy on their hearts, Sira knew that their journey wasn't over. Their relationship, far from smooth sailing, was still navigating stormy seas. But for the first time, they were both facing the storm together, their hands clasped, their hearts intertwined. The path ahead would still be challenging, filled with its share of anxieties and insecurities, but together, they could navigate the rough waters, stronger and more resilient than ever before. The unexpected arrival of Noah, the reason for this crucial conversation, had inadvertently strengthened their bond, revealing the depth of their commitment and paving the way for a deeper, more profound understanding of each other. The future remained uncertain, yet the promise of enduring love and unwavering support shone brightly, a beacon of hope in the sometimes turbulent waters of their shared life.

A Confrontation with the Ex

The following morning, the tension hung heavy in the air, a silent aftermath of Noah's unexpected arrival. Keith, ever the pragmatist, had brushed it off, attributing it to a chance encounter, a harmless coincidence. But Sira knew better. The lingering scent of Noah's cologne, a familiar and subtly intoxicating blend of sandalwood and cedarwood, still clung to her clothes, a phantom touch that stirred a bittersweet ache in her chest. The encounter wasn't a passionate reunion; it was a gentle stirring of memories, a bittersweet reminder of a simpler time, a time before the complexities of adult life, before mortgages and pregnancy tests and the ever-present shadow of Keith's ex-girlfriends.

She found Noah waiting for her outside the coffee shop, a nervous energy radiating from him. He looked different – older, perhaps, with a hint of weariness in his eyes that hadn't been there before. He was dressed casually, a stark contrast to the polished, somewhat preppy image she remembered from high school. He held a small bouquet of sunflowers, their bright faces a stark contrast to the overcast sky.

"Sira," he began, his voice a low murmur, tinged with a nervousness that mirrored her own. "I… I didn't mean to cause any trouble."

"Trouble?" Sira echoed, a small laugh escaping her lips. The word felt oddly inappropriate, given the weight of their past and the uncertainty of their present. "It's not trouble, Noah. It's… complicated."

He nodded, a slight furrow creasing his brow. "I understand. I just… I saw you, and I couldn't help myself. It's been a long time."

They found a quiet corner table, the hum of conversation a distant backdrop to their private exchange. He launched into an explanation, a carefully crafted narrative of his life since their high school graduation. He spoke of college, of his struggles to find his footing, of the various jobs he'd held, of the heartbreak he'd endured. It wasn't a romantic narrative, but a story of perseverance, a testament to his resilience in the face of adversity. He spoke with honesty, a genuine vulnerability that she found surprisingly endearing, a far cry from the confident, somewhat cocky teenager she remembered.

He confessed that he'd moved back to town after a failed attempt at establishing a career in another state. He'd been working for his uncle's construction firm, a far cry from his dreams of becoming a renowned architect, but he was making a decent living, and that was something. He explained that he hadn't intended to intrude on her life, that he had only stopped to say hello, to see how she was. He'd seen her with Keith, and he'd realized, with a pang of regret, how much he'd missed out on.

"I was young and foolish," he admitted, his gaze dropping to his hands. "I didn't know how to handle things, how to handle you. I was scared of commitment, of the responsibility that came with a serious relationship. I took you for granted, and for that, I'm truly sorry."

Sira listened, a complex array of emotions swirling within her. There was guilt, a residue of the past; there was also a surprising sense of peace. Noah's confession wasn't an attempt to rekindle their romance; it was an apology, a sincere expression of remorse. He wasn't trying to win her back; he was simply acknowledging his past mistakes. It was a maturity she hadn't anticipated, a growth that shed light on the reasons for their breakup.

"I was young too," she responded softly, her voice barely a whisper above the low hum of the coffee shop. "We were both figuring things out, making mistakes. It wasn't just you, Noah. I have my own share of regrets."

Their conversation flowed easily after that, a comfortable exchange of memories and experiences. They talked about their families, their friends, their aspirations, the dreams they'd pursued and the ones they'd abandoned. They spoke of shared memories – the awkward high school dances, the late-night study sessions, the stolen kisses under the bleachers. There was a nostalgia in their conversation, a sense of shared history that transcended the years that had passed. It wasn't about romantic longing; it was a connection forged in youth, a bond that time and distance hadn't entirely erased.

But beneath the surface current of reminiscence, a deeper question lingered. The casual nature of their encounter, the absence of any romantic tension, revealed something crucial. Their past was a chapter closed, a story concluded, not an unfinished symphony waiting for a final movement. The Noah she saw before her was not the immature boy who'd walked away from her all those years ago; he was a man who had learned from his mistakes, a man who had found a different path. Seeing this growth, this maturity, released a weight from Sira's shoulders. The guilt that had clung to her since his appearance began to dissipate, replaced by a sense of closure.

As their coffee cups emptied, they fell silent, the only sound the gentle clatter of cutlery from nearby tables. The sun, finally breaking through the clouds, cast a warm glow across the café, illuminating the subtle changes in both their faces. The conversation had been cathartic, a release of pent-up emotions and unspoken words. The meeting hadn't been a threat to her relationship with Keith; it had been a confirmation of her present, a validation of her growth and her choices.

Noah stood up, his smile genuine and devoid of any lingering romantic undertones. "It was good to see you, Sira. Really."

"You too, Noah," she replied, her voice steady and calm. "Take care."

He hesitated for a moment, then leaned in, offering a friendly hug, a simple gesture of farewell, devoid of the passion or longing that had once characterized their embraces. The hug was brief, platonic, a gesture of friendship rather than romance. As he walked away, she felt a pang of sadness, but it wasn't the heart-wrenching sorrow of a lost love; it was the melancholic acceptance of a chapter closed. The past was acknowledged, understood, and finally, released. She watched him go, feeling a sense of peace settle over her, a quiet contentment that had been missing until this unexpected reunion. The conversation with Noah hadn't changed her relationship with Keith; it had, however, helped her to understand herself better, to accept her past, and to move forward with a renewed clarity and a deeper appreciation for the present.

The weight of the previous day's anxieties began to lift. She felt lighter, somehow cleansed. The encounter with Noah hadn't stirred any hidden flames of old romance; instead, it had served as a moment for self-reflection, reinforcing her commitment to her present relationship. It was a reminder of her journey, of her growth, and of the strength she had developed over the years. She realized that the challenges she faced with Keith weren't just about his ex-girlfriends or his perceived lack of understanding; they were about navigating the complex terrain of a long-term relationship, a relationship fraught with its own unique set of difficulties. Noah's unexpected appearance, far from threatening their bond, had ironically strengthened it, helping her to solidify her commitment to Keith and the life they were building together.

The afternoon sunlight streamed through her kitchen window as she prepared lunch, the scent of garlic and herbs filling the air. The quiet hum of the refrigerator was a comforting backdrop to her thoughts. She smiled, a genuine, heartfelt smile that reached her eyes. The encounter with Noah had been an unexpected detour, but it had led her back to the heart of her present, to the reality of her life with Keith, a reality that, despite its challenges, was filled with love, hope, and the promise of a future yet unwritten.

She picked up her phone, the image of Keith's smiling face her phone's background, a silent reassurance of her commitment to him. She texted him, a simple message conveying her intention to be home early, a promise of a quiet evening, an evening filled with the comforting presence of her partner, her lover, the father of her child. The anxieties of the previous day seemed distant now, muted echoes of a storm that had passed, leaving behind a clear, calm sky. The path ahead would still have its challenges, but she was ready to face them, armed with a newfound understanding of herself and an unwavering commitment to the man she loved. The unexpected reunion with Noah had been a poignant reminder of the past, a lesson in growth and acceptance, ultimately leading her back to the present, to the love she cherished, and to the future she was eagerly anticipating. The weight of her pregnancy, the financial pressures, the insecurities surrounding Keith's exes – these were still present, but they were no longer insurmountable obstacles. They were simply challenges to be met, obstacles to be overcome, together.

Navigating the New Dynamic

The evening unfolded with a tentative quiet. Keith, sensing Sira's subdued mood, tried to bridge the gap, offering a gentle hand squeeze as they settled on the sofa. The television flickered, a silent backdrop to their unspoken tension. He'd bought takeout – her favorite Thai – but the aromatic steam seemed to only heighten the palpable unease.

"So," Keith began, his voice hesitant, "about Noah…"

Sira looked up, her gaze meeting his. She'd spent the afternoon wrestling with her feelings, analyzing the encounter, trying to untangle the unexpected knot of emotions it had created. The past, suddenly so vivid, felt like a ghost at the feast, an unwelcome guest at their intimate dinner for two.

"It was… unexpected," she admitted, choosing her words carefully. "But it wasn't… romantic. It was just… a reminder."

"A reminder of what?" Keith pressed, a flicker of possessiveness in his eyes. He didn't want to be insecure, he really didn't, but the shadow of Noah lingered, a subtle discomfort in the otherwise cozy atmosphere. The thought that Sira might still harbor feelings for her high school sweetheart was a bitter pill to swallow.

"Of… a simpler time," Sira replied, avoiding his intense gaze. "Before all this… before the house, before the baby, before… everything." The weight of their current situation pressed down on her, a heavy blanket of responsibility.

Keith nodded slowly, understanding dawning in his eyes. He knew what she meant. Their relationship was a whirlwind – a beautiful, chaotic whirlwind – but it was a far cry from the carefree days of college, the days before the complexities of adult life had descended upon them like a relentless storm.

"I get it," he said softly, reaching out to gently caress her cheek. "But we're here now, together. We're building something... something real."

"I know," Sira whispered, leaning into his touch. The reassurance, however, felt fragile, a delicate butterfly fluttering on the edge of a storm. The shadow of Noah, and the subtle anxieties stirred by the presence of Keith's exes, still threatened to disrupt the delicate balance of their relationship.

The next few days were a delicate dance of communication and compromise. They talked, really talked, not just about the practicalities of impending parenthood and mortgage payments, but about their feelings, their insecurities, their fears. Sira confessed her anxieties about the future, the overwhelming responsibility of raising a child, the constant pressure she felt to manage everything – her emotions, their finances, their relationship. Keith listened, truly listened, his earlier dismissal of her worries replaced with genuine empathy and concern

He, in turn, admitted his own struggles. The casual friendships he maintained with his ex-girlfriends – friendships he'd always considered innocent – now felt different, viewed through the lens of Sira's insecurity. He understood that his casual interactions could be misinterpreted, that his casual tone and nonchalant attitude could be hurting her. He pledged to be more mindful, more considerate, to make an extra effort to make her feel secure and loved.

The three-way dynamic – Sira, Keith, and the lingering presence of his exes – proved to be unexpectedly challenging. Sira found herself navigating a complex emotional landscape, her feelings fluctuating between insecurity, jealousy, and a deep-seated fear of abandonment. She realized that her anxieties weren't simply about Noah's reappearance, but stemmed from deeper, more profound insecurities about her worthiness, her ability to be enough for Keith, and her capabilities as a future mother.

One afternoon, while Keith was at work, Sira received a text from Chloe, one of Keith's ex-girlfriends. It was a simple, innocuous message – an invitation to a coffee date. Sira's immediate reaction was a surge of jealousy, a possessive instinct she hadn't anticipated. She was surprised by the intensity of the emotion.

She considered ignoring the text, but decided against it. Instead, she texted Keith, sharing the message and confessing her feelings. Keith's response was immediate and reassuring. He understood her discomfort, and he offered to call Chloe and set the record straight, reassuring her that he had no intention of betraying Sira's trust. He understood Sira's anxiety now, and was making an effort to address the root cause.

This small act of transparency and open communication proved to be a turning point. Sira realized that Keith's commitment to their relationship was genuine, that his friendships with his exes weren't a threat, but a reflection of his ability to maintain healthy relationships with people from his past.

The arrival of their child further solidified their bond. The shared responsibility, the sleepless nights, the overwhelming joy of parenthood forged a new level of intimacy and understanding. Sira's anxieties didn't completely disappear, but they were now tempered by a deep sense of security and trust in Keith's love and commitment.

However, the challenges persisted. Navigating the complexities of parenthood and the financial strain of their new life together proved to be a constant test of their resilience and commitment. They learned to rely on each other, to lean on each other during tough times, to celebrate each small victory together. They were learning to become a family, a unit, stronger together than they could ever be apart.

The unexpected reunion with Noah had served as a spark, forcing them to confront their insecurities and work through the underlying issues that threatened their relationship. It had shaken their foundation, but it also made them stronger. They had learned to communicate, to compromise, to trust each other implicitly. The path ahead was still uncertain, filled with unexpected twists and turns, but they were ready to face them, together. They were a team, a family in the making, their love a resilient flame burning brightly in the face of life's challenges.

The arrival of their daughter, Maya, brought a wave of overwhelming love and a profound sense of purpose. The anxieties surrounding Keith's ex-girlfriends faded into the background, replaced by the urgent demands and joys of parenthood. Sira, initially overwhelmed by the responsibility, found a newfound strength and confidence in her ability to nurture and protect her child. Keith, equally invested, blossomed into a devoted father, his earlier insecurities replaced by a deep and abiding love for his family.

Their financial struggles continued, but they faced them as a united front, learning to budget, to prioritize, and to rely on each other's support. The weight of their mortgage and the ever-increasing expenses of raising a child were significant, but the bond they shared transcended material possessions. Their love story wasn't just about a fairytale romance; it was a testament to their resilience, their commitment, and their ability to overcome life's challenges together.

Years passed. Maya grew, their relationship deepened. The unexpected reunion with Noah remained a distant memory, a poignant reminder of a simpler time. Sira and Keith's story was a living example that true love isn't about avoiding conflict or challenges, but about facing them head-on, together. They had built a life, a family, a love that stood the test of time, a love forged in the fires of adversity and strengthened by the unwavering commitment they shared. Their journey was far from over, but they were ready, hand in hand, to face whatever the future held, knowing that together, they were unstoppable. The anxieties, the insecurities, the uncertainties of the past had paved the way for a deeper, more profound love, a love that only time and shared experiences could strengthen. Their story was a testament to the enduring power of love, a love that not only survived the challenges but emerged stronger, more resilient, and more deeply rooted than ever before.

Chapter 5

Repairing Broken Trust

The silence in the car was thick, heavy with the unspoken accusations and lingering anxieties. The drive home from the chance encounter with Noah, Sira's high school sweetheart, felt longer than it actually was. Keith's knuckles were white, gripping the steering wheel so tightly his joints were visibly straining. He hadn't spoken a word since Noah had walked away, leaving Sira seemingly unaffected but actually reeling internally.

Sira, meanwhile, felt a familiar knot of guilt twisting in her stomach. She hadn't meant for the encounter to happen; it had been a completely chance meeting at the coffee shop, a fleeting moment that had stretched into an awkward, fifteen-minute conversation about old times and the paths their lives had taken. Noah had been charming, even more so than she remembered, and the casual reminiscing had felt oddly comfortable, a stark contrast to the tense atmosphere she now shared with Keith.

"He just… asked how I was doing," Sira finally said, her voice barely a whisper, breaking the heavy silence. She watched Keith's profile, the rigid set of his jaw a testament to his simmering unease.

Keith finally turned, his gaze intense. "Asked how you were doing? Is that all? He didn't mention the… the things you two used to do? The things you never told me about?" His voice was tight, laced with barely suppressed anger.

The accusation hung in the air, a sharp, painful jab. Sira winced. "There's nothing to tell, Keith. It was high school. We were kids. It's over."

"But it wasn't over for him , was it?" Keith challenged, his voice rising slightly. "He clearly still has feelings for you."

Sira sighed, feeling the familiar exhaustion settle over her. This was exactly the conversation she'd been dreading, the one that threatened to unravel everything they had worked so hard to build. "He was just being polite, Keith. He's got a girlfriend now. A fiancé, actually. He even mentioned her."

Keith's jaw clenched again. "Polite? He was lingering, Sira. He was looking at you like…" He trailed off, unable to articulate the unspoken threat he felt. The insecurity he felt was palpable, a tangible presence in the small space of the car.

The truth was, Keith's jealousy was a raw nerve, a constant undercurrent in their relationship that had been aggravated by the stress of Sira's pregnancy and their ongoing financial struggles. Sira knew that his anxieties stemmed from a place of deep love and fear of losing her, but it still hurt. It felt like his insecurity was constantly casting a shadow over their relationship, an unspoken accusation that she would inevitably betray him.

"I understand you're worried," Sira said softly, reaching out to touch his arm. He flinched away, his body language speaking volumes about his turmoil. She pulled her hand back, a pang of sadness cutting through her. "But I'm not going to leave you, Keith. Noah is just… a ghost from my past. He doesn't matter. You're the only one who matters."

The words hung in the air, heavy with the weight of her sincerity. The statement, however simple, required a leap of faith from Keith, a decision to believe her despite the unsettling encounter. It took a moment, a long, agonizing moment filled with the rhythmic thump of Keith's heart pounding against his ribs, before he finally nodded, his eyes filled with a mixture of relief and lingering doubt.

"I know," he whispered, his voice barely audible. "But it's hard, Sira. It's really hard."

That night, after a quiet dinner where the conversation was strained but civil, Keith initiated a conversation that felt different. It was less about blame and more about vulnerability, a tentative step towards a deeper level of understanding.

"I've been thinking," Keith began, picking at his food, "about all this… the ex-girlfriends, Noah, everything. I've been acting like a jerk."

Sira looked up, surprised by his directness. His admission felt like a breakthrough, a crack in the wall of mistrust that had been building between them.

"I'm insecure," he continued, his voice low and hesitant. "I'm terrified of losing you. The pregnancy, the house, the money… it's all so much. And seeing Noah… it just brought all those fears to the surface."

Sira reached across the table, taking his hand in hers. "I know," she said, her voice gentle. "And I'm sorry. I haven't been the easiest person to deal with either. The hormones, the anxiety... it's all been a lot."

For the next hour, they talked, truly talked, not just exchanging words but sharing emotions. Keith admitted to his past anxieties regarding relationships, his fear of abandonment rooted in his childhood experiences. Sira shared her own insecurities, her worries about being a good mother, her fear of failing in her responsibilities.

They talked about trust, about communication, about the importance of vulnerability in a relationship. They discussed ways to improve, to better understand each other's needs and anxieties. The conversation was raw and honest, a painful but necessary process of peeling back layers of resentment and fear to reveal the love that still burned beneath the surface.

Over the following weeks, the efforts to repair the broken trust were a continuous process. Keith made a conscious effort to manage his jealousy, acknowledging his insecurities instead of projecting them onto Sira. He started spending less time with his ex-girlfriends, understanding that it caused Sira pain, even if the friendships were purely platonic. He sought to reassure her of his commitment, both verbally and through actions. He helped with the chores, listened to her anxieties, and provided emotional support.

Sira, in turn, worked on improving her communication, being more upfront about her feelings and anxieties, instead of bottling them up and letting them fester. She initiated conversations, expressing her needs and her anxieties. She made an effort to be more understanding of Keith's insecurities, recognizing that his jealousy wasn't malicious, but a manifestation of his love and concern.

Their therapy sessions became a crucial part of their healing process. The therapist helped them identify their communication patterns, learn to express their feelings constructively, and develop coping mechanisms for handling conflict and stress. They learned about healthy relationship dynamics, communication skills, and how to navigate difficult situations without resorting to accusations or blame.

The journey wasn't easy. There were still moments of tension, of misunderstandings, and even occasional flare-ups of old anxieties. But each time, they approached the conflict differently. They used their newfound communication skills to address the issues head-on, expressing their needs and feelings honestly and respectfully. They actively listened to each other, validating each other's emotions, and working together to find solutions that worked for both of them. They focused on building a foundation of mutual respect, understanding, and empathy.

Gradually, the cracks in their relationship began to mend. The constant tension eased, replaced by a growing sense of security and trust. The fear that had once dominated their interactions started to fade, replaced by a burgeoning confidence in their ability to overcome obstacles together. Their love, tested and refined by the challenges they faced, emerged stronger and deeper than before. The future still held uncertainties, the anxieties surrounding the impending arrival of their child remained, but now, they faced them together, hand-in-hand, ready to navigate whatever came their way. The encounter with Noah, while initially devastating, had ultimately served as a catalyst for significant growth and a renewed commitment to their relationship. It forced them to confront their weaknesses, to address their unspoken fears, and ultimately, to emerge from the experience stronger and more unified than ever before. The road ahead would undoubtedly present further challenges, but they had learned a valuable lesson about the importance of communication, vulnerability, and the unwavering power of mutual trust in a relationship.

Open Communication and Vulnerability

The quiet hum of the refrigerator was the only sound in the otherwise still kitchen. Sira, perched on a stool at the counter, absently peeled an orange, the vibrant segments a stark contrast to the muted grayness of the morning light. Keith entered, the scent of coffee clinging to him like a second skin. He moved towards her, a hesitant gentleness in his movements that was a far cry from the rigid tension of the previous days.

"Morning," he murmured, his voice still carrying a trace of the strain that had settled upon him after Noah's unexpected appearance.

Sira offered a small smile, a flicker of warmth in the cool atmosphere. "Morning." She popped an orange segment into her mouth, the sweetness a momentary distraction from the weight of their unspoken anxieties.

The silence stretched, comfortable yet charged with the unspoken understanding that hung between them. It wasn't the strained silence of accusation, but rather the quiet contemplation of a shared experience, a shared vulnerability. It was the kind of silence that allowed for the slow, steady mending of a fractured connection, the unspoken language of two souls trying to find their way back to each other.

Keith pulled out a chair, settling across from her. He watched her for a moment, his gaze lingering on the delicate curve of her jaw, the slight tremor in her hand as she continued to peel the orange. He saw the fatigue etched into her face, the quiet exhaustion that lay beneath her carefully constructed composure. He knew she was carrying the weight of the world on her shoulders, a burden he'd inadvertently added to with his own anxieties and insecurities.

He cleared his throat, the sound breaking the spell of quiet observation. "I... I'm sorry, Sira," he began, his voice low and hesitant. "About Noah. About everything."

Sira looked up, her eyes meeting his. There was no anger in her gaze, only a weariness that mirrored his own. "It's not just Noah, Keith," she said softly, her voice barely a whisper. "It's everything. The house, the money, the pregnancy... It's all just... overwhelming."

The dam finally broke. The carefully constructed walls of composure crumbled, revealing the raw vulnerability beneath. Tears welled in Sira's eyes, escaping to trace paths down her cheeks. Keith reached across the counter, his hand covering hers. His touch was gentle, reassuring, a silent promise of support.

"I know," he said, his voice thick with emotion. "I know it's overwhelming. And I've been... a jerk. I haven't been there for you like I should have been. I let my insecurities get the better of me. I jumped to conclusions, made assumptions… I didn't listen."

Sira leaned into his touch, her tears flowing freely now. "I know you were scared, Keith," she whispered. "Scared of losing your friends, scared of me changing, scared of everything changing."

"And I was wrong," Keith said firmly, his voice regaining its strength. "Terribly wrong. I should have trusted you. I should have had faith in us."

They sat in silence for a long moment, the quiet punctuated only by Sira's soft sobs. It was a silence filled with remorse, with understanding, with the beginnings of healing. It was a silence that allowed them to fully acknowledge the depth of their pain, their fears, and their profound love for each other.

"I felt so alone," Sira confessed, her voice catching in her throat. "Like you were pulling away, and I had no one to turn to. Even my own family is miles away."

Keith pulled her close, enveloping her in a hug that spoke volumes of unspoken apologies and unwavering support. "You're not alone, Sira. You never will be. I'm here. Always."

It wasn't a magical cure-all, a sudden erasure of their problems. Their challenges remained – the financial strain, the anxieties surrounding the pregnancy, the lingering shadows of Keith's past relationships. But something fundamental had shifted. The walls of silence had been broken down, replaced by a raw, honest vulnerability that allowed them to truly see and understand each other.

The following days were a slow, deliberate process of rebuilding. They talked, endlessly, tirelessly, about everything and nothing. They talked about Noah, and Keith's lingering insecurities, and the sheer terror of becoming parents. Sira shared her fears about her changing body, the anxieties of childbirth, and the overwhelming responsibility that lay ahead. Keith, in turn, confessed his apprehension about fatherhood, his worry about not being a good enough provider, his concern that he'd somehow fail Sira and their child.

They attended couples therapy, a decision they both initially resisted but ultimately embraced as a vital tool for strengthening their communication and resolving their conflicts. The therapist helped them navigate their anxieties, learn healthy conflict resolution techniques, and cultivate a more profound understanding of each other's emotional needs.

Through therapy, Sira discovered that her anxieties weren't simply a reaction to Keith's behavior. They were rooted in deeper insecurities about her own self-worth and her ability to handle the responsibilities of adulthood. She had always been a highly independent person, but the sudden weight of pregnancy, coupled with financial instability, had shaken her sense of self. Keith, for his part, acknowledged his own self-doubt and his tendency towards emotional distancing.

They learned to identify their triggers, to express their needs without resorting to accusatory language, and to listen empathetically to each other's concerns. They began practicing active listening, reflecting back what each other said to ensure they understood each other's perspectives. They agreed to create weekly "check-in" times to discuss their feelings, anxieties, and challenges, a regular space dedicated solely to open and honest communication.

Keith made a concerted effort to communicate more openly about his anxieties and insecurities. He no longer attempted to downplay his feelings or brush them under the rug. He actively sought Sira's understanding and support, sharing his fears and vulnerabilities without reservation.

Sira learned to articulate her own needs more assertively, without feeling guilty or demanding. She understood that expressing her vulnerabilities wasn't a sign of weakness, but a sign of strength, a testament to her willingness to build a stronger, more authentic relationship with Keith.

The transformation wasn't instantaneous. There were still moments of frustration, moments of disagreement, and moments where old patterns threatened to resurface. But now, they had the tools, the willingness, and the unwavering commitment to navigate these challenges together. They had discovered the transformative power of open communication and vulnerability, transforming what could have been a destructive pattern into a foundation for a stronger, more resilient relationship.

Their journey wasn't just about resolving their current crisis; it was about laying the groundwork for a lifetime of honest and open communication. It was about learning to navigate the complexities of adult life together, to face the challenges of parenthood as a united front, and to build a future based on mutual respect, unwavering trust, and the unshakeable bond forged in the crucible of vulnerability. The encounter with Noah had been a catalyst, forcing them to confront their unspoken fears and anxieties. But it was the subsequent journey of open communication and shared vulnerability that truly strengthened their relationship, forging a bond that was stronger, deeper, and infinitely more resilient than before. They had finally learned to truly trust each other, not just with words, but with their hearts.

Understanding Past Relationships

The scent of freshly brewed coffee still hung in the air, a faint but persistent reminder of the tense morning that had passed. Sira, having finished her orange, now idly traced patterns on the condensation forming on her glass. The quiet, however, felt different now, charged with a newfound understanding that had blossomed from their late-night conversation. Noah's unexpected appearance had served as a catalyst, forcing them to confront not just their present anxieties but also the shadows cast by their pasts.

Keith broke the silence, his voice soft, almost hesitant. "About Noah… I didn't know you were that close to him." He wasn't accusatory; rather, his tone held a genuine curiosity, a desire to understand the depth of Sira's past.

Sira sighed, a small exhale that seemed to carry the weight of years. "It was high school, Keith. We were young, naive. It was intense, passionate… but also incredibly immature." She paused, swirling the ice in her glass. "We broke up because we were simply incompatible. Different paths, different dreams. There was no cheating, no betrayal, just… growth. We've both changed so much since then." She looked at him directly, her gaze unwavering. "He was my first love, but he's not the love of my life. You are."

Keith reached across the counter, his hand covering hers. His touch was reassuring, grounding. "I know," he murmured, his thumb gently stroking her knuckles. "But knowing that doesn't erase the insecurity, you know? Seeing him… it stirred things up." He confessed, his honesty raw and vulnerable. "I've never been good at sharing you. I guess that's partly why I reacted so defensively when your pregnancy was announced. Part of me felt like you were pulling away, trying to create distance."

Sira nodded, understanding dawning in her eyes. "And my insecurities about your ex-girlfriends? They're real, Keith. Seeing you still friendly with them… it makes me wonder if I'm enough. If I measure up."

The admission hung in the air, heavy with unspoken fears and insecurities. They sat in comfortable silence for a while, each contemplating their own anxieties and vulnerabilities. The conversation was a testament to their growing maturity, their willingness to delve into the complex emotions that shaped their relationship. The conversation moved on to the past relationships.

Keith began to speak about his past relationships, starting with his first serious girlfriend, Chloe. He described her as vibrant and outgoing, the opposite of his reserved nature. Their relationship, he admitted, had been a whirlwind of passionate moments and fiery arguments. The breakup, he explained, was mutual, but tinged with a lingering sense of loss and regret. He admitted that he hadn't always handled the breakup maturely and had struggled with maintaining a healthy distance afterwards.

"Chloe was the first person I truly loved," Keith confessed, his voice low. "Losing her was like losing a part of myself. I learned a lot from that relationship, though. I learned about communication, or rather, the lack of it. We were too stubborn, too focused on proving our points instead of listening. It taught me the importance of compromise, of understanding each other's perspectives."

Sira listened intently, her heart aching with empathy. She understood the complexities of heartbreak, the way past relationships could leave an indelible mark on the soul. She had her own stories of past relationships, some more significant than others. There was Mark, a college sweetheart who had been her steadfast companion for two years. Their relationship ended due to distance after Mark secured an internship on the other side of the country. They tried to make it work, but the strain of long-distance eventually proved too much.

"Mark," Sira began, her voice soft. "He was my comfort, my safe place. He wasn't the fiery passion of Noah, but a gentle, steady hand that held mine through tough times. But even the steadiest hands can't always bridge the miles."

There was also Daniel, a brief encounter that felt more like a chapter in a book that Sira had long since closed. Daniel had been charming and intelligent but ultimately emotionally unavailable. Their relationship had never been serious, but it had taught Sira the importance of open communication and emotional maturity in a partner.

As they continued to share, the weight of their pasts eased. The stories weren't just a recounting of past mistakes; they were a map, charting their emotional growth and highlighting the lessons they'd learned. They saw in each other's past experiences a reflection of their own journeys, a validation of the struggles and triumphs that shaped who they were today.

The conversation wasn't just about recounting past relationships; it was about understanding the impact of those experiences on their present dynamic. Keith realized the depth of Sira's anxieties stemmed not from a desire to control him, but from her own vulnerabilities. His past relationships, while seemingly resolved, had left him with insecurities of his own. He realized his defensiveness towards her pregnancy wasn't just about protecting his friendships; it was also about protecting himself from the fear of another painful loss.

Sira, in turn, gained a deeper understanding of Keith's emotional landscape. His seemingly casual friendships with his ex-girlfriends were rooted in a desire to maintain positive relationships, not an attempt to undermine their commitment. She understood his initial reaction to her pregnancy as a manifestation of his own fears and anxieties. It wasn't a rejection of her or their child, but rather a desperate attempt to grapple with the monumental changes occurring in his life.

Their conversation extended late into the night, fueled by honesty and mutual empathy. They discussed their hopes and dreams for the future, the challenges they anticipated, and the unwavering commitment they both felt towards their relationship. The shared vulnerability built a bridge between their pasts and their future, strengthening their bond in ways they had never imagined possible.

The talk wasn't just about the past relationships; it also delved into the nature of trust and honesty within their current relationship. They discussed their individual communication styles, acknowledging their strengths and weaknesses. Sira admitted to being sometimes guarded, a consequence of past hurt, while Keith confessed to needing time to process his emotions, sometimes leading to silence where words were needed.

Their discussions were infused with a sense of hope, a sense of renewal. The weight of anxieties and insecurities that had clouded their relationship was beginning to dissipate, replaced by a clearer, more profound understanding of each other. They agreed to make conscious efforts to improve their communication, scheduling regular "check-in" times to openly discuss their feelings and anxieties. They even created a shared online document where they could write down their worries and concerns, eliminating the pressure of immediate verbal confrontation.

The house, initially a source of contention, became a symbol of their shared future. They spent the next few days selecting paint colors, discussing furniture arrangements, and making plans to decorate the nursery. Each decision was a small act of cooperation, a testament to their growing unity. The process itself became a journey of shared responsibility, an affirmation of their love and commitment.

The conversation evolved beyond just their past relationships and delved into the larger spectrum of their lives. They discussed their career aspirations, their long-term financial goals, and their visions for raising their child. Sira's apprehensions about balancing her career and motherhood were addressed with empathy and understanding, leading to practical solutions and shared responsibilities. Keith, for example, offered to manage household chores more proactively, recognizing the importance of equitable distribution of responsibilities.

Their journey wasn't just about understanding their individual pasts; it was about co-creating a shared narrative for their future, a future built on a foundation of unshakeable trust and unwavering honesty. They were still a work in progress, their relationship continuously evolving and adapting, but the shared vulnerability and honest communication had created a space where they could navigate the complexities of life together, hand in hand. The past was no longer a shadowy specter haunting their present, but a source of learning and growth that fueled their love and strengthened their bond. The surprise encounter with Noah had indeed been a catalyst, but the real transformation had occurred in the crucible of their subsequent conversations, where honesty and understanding forged a future they could both envision and confidently embrace. The future held many challenges, but now, together, they were ready to face them, fortified by a love that had grown stronger through the crucible of understanding.

Addressing Keiths Jealousy

The afternoon sun cast long shadows across the living room, painting the newly purchased house in a warm, golden hue. Sira sat curled on the sofa, a half-finished book resting on her lap, her mind miles away. The conversation with Noah had hung in the air like a lingering scent, a stark reminder of the insecurities that still simmered beneath the surface of their relationship. Keith, sensing her quiet contemplation, approached cautiously. He sat beside her, his arm gently brushing hers.

"Thinking about Noah?" he asked softly, his voice tinged with a vulnerability Sira hadn't seen before.

Sira nodded, a small sigh escaping her lips. "A little," she admitted. "It just... brought everything back. All those things I hadn't really processed."

"I know," Keith replied, his gaze meeting hers. "And I'm sorry. I haven't been... easy to be with lately. The jealousy, the insecurity... it's been eating me alive."

He confessed to feelings he hadn't allowed himself to articulate before. The fear of losing Sira, the fear of not being enough, the gnawing uncertainty fueled by the constant presence of his friendly exes – it all poured out in a torrent of raw emotion. He spoke of the pressure he felt to be the perfect partner, the perfect provider, the perfect everything. The weight of buying the house, of supporting Sira and their unborn child, pressed down on him, exacerbating his already simmering insecurities. He admitted he'd felt threatened by Noah's reappearance, not because he doubted Sira's love, but because the past had unearthed old wounds he hadn't fully healed.

Sira listened patiently, her hand finding his. She understood the pressure he was under, the anxieties that gnawed at him. She knew that his jealousy wasn't a reflection of her actions, but rather a symptom of his own internal struggles. She'd seen the strain on him, the way his shoulders tightened when he saw her talking to other men, even just casually. The way his eyes would cloud over with a mixture of possessiveness and fear. She'd always attributed it to his protective nature, but now she saw the deeper roots of his insecurity.

"It's not just Noah, is it?" Sira asked gently. "It's… everything, isn't it? The house, the baby, the other girls… It's all piling up."

Keith nodded, tears welling in his eyes. "I feel like I'm drowning," he confessed, his voice thick with emotion. "I love you more than anything, Sira. More than I ever thought possible. But this… this jealousy, it's consuming me."

Sira held his hand tighter, offering him comfort and reassurance, he desperately needed it. She understood. She too felt the weight of their situation, the overwhelming responsibility of navigating adulthood and parenthood while battling their individual demons. But she also knew that their love was strong enough to weather this storm.

"We'll face this together," she said, her voice firm but gentle. "We'll find a way to work through it. But you have to let me help you."

That night, after a quiet dinner and a long, comforting hug, Keith agreed to seek professional help. He admitted that he needed guidance to manage his jealousy in a healthy way, to understand its roots and develop coping mechanisms. He knew that his behavior wasn't fair to Sira, and he was determined to change.

The following weeks were a journey of self-discovery for Keith. He started therapy, initially hesitant and resistant, but gradually opening up to the process. He learned to identify his triggers, to understand the patterns of his behavior, and to develop strategies for managing his emotions. His therapist helped him understand that his jealousy wasn't a reflection of Sira's character, but rather a manifestation of his own insecurities and fears of abandonment stemming from his childhood.

He learned to communicate his feelings without resorting to accusations or controlling behaviors. He learned to trust Sira, to believe in her love and commitment, and to let go of the need to constantly monitor or control her actions. He started to appreciate the importance of healthy boundaries, recognizing that respecting Sira's independence didn't diminish his love for her, but rather strengthened it.

He began to see his past relationships in a new light, understanding that the amicable relationships he maintained with his exes weren't a threat to his present relationship with Sira, but rather a testament to his ability to maintain healthy relationships. He started to understand that his previous relationships, positive and negative, taught him valuable life lessons and shaped him into the person he was today. He learned to trust that his past didn't define his future, and that he could choose to build a secure and loving relationship based on mutual respect and trust.

The process wasn't easy. There were moments of relapse, moments where his old insecurities threatened to resurface. But with each setback, Keith learned to identify his triggers and actively work on his responses. Sira was a constant source of support and encouragement, patiently guiding him through his journey, offering unwavering love and understanding. She too, was growing and evolving, learning to recognize and address her own anxieties and insecurities.

One evening, while strolling hand-in-hand through their neighborhood park, Keith looked at Sira, a genuine smile playing on his lips. "Remember those first few weeks after we moved in?" he asked, his voice filled with a newfound lightness. "I was a mess, wasn't I?"

Sira chuckled. "A little," she admitted, gently squeezing his hand.

"I was so consumed by my own insecurities," he continued. "I let my jealousy dictate my actions, and I hurt you in the process. I'm so sorry."

"I know," Sira said, her voice soft. "But you're working on it. You're getting better. And that's all that matters."

Keith leaned down and kissed her, a deep, heartfelt kiss that spoke volumes. It was a kiss of forgiveness, of understanding, of unwavering love. It was a kiss that signified the end of a difficult chapter and the beginning of a new one, a chapter filled with hope, trust, and unwavering commitment. Their journey had been far from smooth, but they had navigated the rocky terrain together, emerging stronger and more united than ever before. The future still held uncertainties, the challenges of parenthood and adult life looming on the horizon, but now, they faced them not as individuals, but as a team, their love a beacon guiding them through the storms. The house, once a symbol of their financial struggles and Keith's insecurities, now stood as a testament to their resilience, their love a sturdy foundation upon which they were building their future, together. The specter of jealousy still lingered, a shadow of their past, but it no longer held the same power over them. They had learned to confront it, to understand it, to control it; and they were ready to face whatever life threw their way, hand in hand, ready to embrace the future with an unwavering belief in their love and the strength of their bond. The weight of their shared journey had forged them into a stronger, more resilient couple, ready to build a future filled with love, understanding, and unshakeable trust.

Sira's Self-Discovery

The following days were a blur of nesting instincts and emotional introspection. The overwhelming relief of Keith's understanding, the passionate reconciliation, had left Sira with a strange sense of quiet. It wasn't the explosive happiness she'd expected; it was a deeper, more settled calm, laced with a newfound awareness of herself. The pregnancy hormones, she suspected, were playing a part, but something else was shifting within her, a subtle but significant change in her perspective.

She found herself spending more time alone, not in solitude, but in quiet contemplation. The house, once a source of anxiety, now felt like a sanctuary. She explored each room, slowly, deliberately, touching the walls, arranging the furniture, making it their space, their home. It wasn't just about creating a physical space for a baby; it was about creating a space for herself, a space where she could unravel the complexities of her emotions and truly understand her needs.

Her therapist, Dr. Anya Sharma, had been instrumental in this journey. Their sessions weren't about dissecting Keith's flaws or analyzing Noah's surprise visit. Instead, Dr. Sharma gently guided Sira towards self-reflection. She encouraged her to explore her insecurities, not to fix them, but to understand their origins and learn to manage them. Sira realized that her anxieties weren't solely about Keith's past relationships; they stemmed from a deeper wellspring of self-doubt, a fear of not being enough.

"You've always been a people-pleaser, Sira," Dr. Sharma had observed one afternoon, her voice calm and insightful. "You prioritize the needs of others above your own, often neglecting your own feelings and desires. This isn't a bad thing inherently, but it can lead to resentment and insecurity if it's not balanced."

Sira had been stunned. She hadn't consciously realized the extent to which she suppressed her own needs. She had always been the supportive friend, the accommodating girlfriend, the dependable daughter. Her identity was largely defined by her roles in relation to others, leaving little room for her own individuality.

The realization hit her with the force of a tidal wave. She spent hours journaling, pouring out her thoughts and feelings, examining her past relationships, and identifying patterns of self-sacrifice. She analyzed her friendships, her family dynamics, her professional life, recognizing the recurring theme of prioritizing others above herself.

This self-reflection wasn't easy. It involved confronting painful memories, acknowledging past hurts, and accepting that she had often compromised her own happiness to maintain harmony. It was a painful process of peeling back layers of ingrained behavior, uncovering deep-seated beliefs about her worth and her place in the world.

One evening, while Keith was out, Sira revisited old photos. She found pictures from her high school years, images of a younger, more carefree Sira. She had been vibrant, confident, filled with a sense of self that had gradually diminished over the years. She saw herself in school plays, actively involved in clubs, unafraid to express her individuality. Where had that girl gone?

The answer, she realized, was gradual erosion. A subtle shift in priorities, a slow surrender of her own ambitions and dreams to accommodate the expectations of others. The pressure to conform, the desire to please, had slowly but surely chipped away at her sense of self, leaving her feeling lost and insecure.

Understanding this helped Sira define what she needed from Keith, and, more importantly, what she needed from herself. She recognized that her anxieties weren't solely a response to Keith's ex-girlfriends. They were a symptom of her own internal struggles, a manifestation of her long-neglected self. She needed to reclaim that lost sense of self, to rediscover the vibrant young woman she once was.

This newfound self-awareness didn't magically resolve all her insecurities, but it gave her the tools to manage them. She started small, setting boundaries, asserting her needs, and prioritizing her own well-being. She joined a pottery class, something she had always wanted to do but had put off due to other commitments. She reconnected with old friends, allowing herself to be vulnerable and authentic.

The pottery class was particularly transformative. The focus on creating something tangible, on expressing herself through clay, was incredibly therapeutic. It was a physical manifestation of her internal journey, a process of shaping and molding her own identity. The imperfections in her work mirrored the imperfections in herself, but instead of feeling ashamed, she embraced them, recognizing them as part of her unique story.

The conversations with Keith became deeper, more honest, more intimate. She wasn't just sharing her anxieties; she was sharing her aspirations, her dreams, her vulnerabilities. She spoke openly about her past, not to blame him or to elicit sympathy, but to create a deeper understanding between them. She communicated her needs clearly, without fear of judgment or rejection.

Keith, to his credit, listened. He didn't dismiss her feelings or try to fix her problems. He listened with empathy, with love, and with a genuine desire to understand. He asked questions, offering support and encouragement, but he didn't try to control her journey. He understood that her self-discovery was her own process, and his role was to be present, to support her, and to love her unconditionally.

He even started attending therapy sessions with her, not as a requirement, but as an act of solidarity. He wanted to understand her perspective, to learn how to better support her, and to ensure their relationship was built on mutual respect and understanding. Seeing him participate, not just passively listening, was profoundly moving for Sira. It wasn't about fixing her, but about both of them growing together.

The pregnancy itself became a catalyst for this self-discovery. It wasn't just about preparing for a baby; it was about preparing for motherhood, for a new phase of life, with a renewed sense of self. She realized that she couldn't be a good mother if she didn't first take care of herself. She had to prioritize her own physical and emotional health to be able to nurture and care for her child.

This journey wasn't a linear path. There were setbacks, moments of doubt, and times when old insecurities resurfaced. But with each challenge, Sira felt stronger, more resilient, more confident in herself. The initial shock and anxiety surrounding Noah's visit had faded, replaced by a sense of clarity and self-assurance. She understood that her anxieties were hers to manage; they weren't a reflection of Keith's actions or those of anyone else.

The house, once a symbol of their financial struggles, now represented their shared journey, their resilience, their unwavering commitment to each other. It was a testament to their growth, their ability to navigate challenges, and their unwavering love. It was home, not just a place to live, but a haven of love, support, and understanding, built on a foundation of trust and honesty, a testament to their shared journey of self-discovery. The future still held uncertainties, the challenges of parenthood looming large, but they faced them together, hand in hand, their love a beacon guiding them through the unknown. The shadow of jealousy still lingered occasionally, but now, it held far less power. They had learned to understand its roots, and together, they were ready to face any storm, their bond strengthened by their shared journey of self-discovery and unwavering commitment.

Chapter 6

Prenatal Care and Challenges

The first trimester was a blur of nausea, exhaustion, and an overwhelming sense of responsibility. Sira, usually so vibrant and energetic, found herself perpetually tired, her once-sharp wit dulled by a persistent wave of fatigue. Even the simplest tasks felt monumental, leaving her feeling overwhelmed and inadequate. The morning sickness, though not as debilitating as some women experienced, was a constant companion, a reminder of the profound changes occurring within her body. The constant trips to the bathroom, the sudden bouts of dizziness, the overwhelming need to rest – it all felt like a foreign invasion of her normally independent and capable self.

Keith, bless his heart, tried his best. He brought her ginger ale and crackers at 3 AM, rubbed her back when the nausea was particularly bad, and even attempted to learn the intricacies of prenatal vitamins and folic acid. But his attempts at help often fell short. He didn't understand the emotional rollercoaster she was on – the fluctuating hormones, the fear of the unknown, the sheer weight of bringing a new life into the world. He saw the physical symptoms, the fatigue, the morning sickness, but he couldn't fully grasp the internal chaos raging within her.

Their therapist, Dr. Anya Sharma, proved invaluable during this time. She helped Sira navigate the emotional complexities of pregnancy, providing a safe space to express her fears and anxieties without judgment. Sira discovered that many of her anxieties stemmed not just from the pregnancy itself, but also from a deep-seated fear of failure. She worried about being a good mother, a capable partner, and a successful individual all at once. Dr. Sharma helped her unpack these fears, encouraging her to focus on one step at a time, to celebrate small victories, and to accept that it was okay to not have all the answers.

The prenatal appointments became a source of both excitement and trepidation. Each ultrasound was a breathtaking glimpse into the developing life within her, a tangible manifestation of their love and commitment. But with each appointment came a fresh wave of anxieties: Was the baby growing properly? Were there any potential complications? Would she be a good mother? The questions swirled relentlessly in her mind, a constant hum of uncertainty that only deepened as her pregnancy progressed.

The second trimester brought a welcome respite from the morning sickness, but new challenges emerged. Back pain became a constant companion, sleep remained elusive, and the weight gain, though expected, was a source of insecurity for Sira, who had always prided herself on her physique. She found herself avoiding mirrors, feeling self-conscious and awkward in her changing body. Keith's unwavering support helped, though. He reminded her of her beauty, not just in her physical form, but in her strength and resilience. He encouraged her to embrace her pregnant body, celebrating the life blossoming within her.

    Their preparations for the baby's arrival were a blend of excitement and practical planning. They painted the nursery a soft, calming blue, assembling the crib and changing table with a mix of anticipation and nervous energy. They chose names, debating for hours over the perfect fit for their little one. They researched baby products, comparing cribs, strollers, and car seats with the meticulous attention of seasoned shoppers. Sira spent hours meticulously organizing tiny clothes, socks, and blankets, while Keith tackled the more cumbersome tasks – assembling furniture, installing baby gates, and setting up the baby monitor.

    Their families became increasingly involved, their excitement palpable as the due date drew closer. Sira's mother, a kind and supportive woman, visited frequently, sharing stories of her own pregnancy and offering practical advice, while Keith's parents, equally supportive, helped with house renovations and shopping. The sense of community and support surrounding them was a vital buffer against the anxieties of impending parenthood. The conversations often centered on parenthood, each sharing stories and concerns, anxieties and expectations, creating a collective learning experience.

The couple's relationship shifted too. As Sira's body changed, so did the intimacy between them. Their physical connection adapted, evolving from passionate embraces to gentler caresses and moments of shared quietude. Sira often felt vulnerable and self-conscious about her changing body, but Keith's unwavering support helped her embrace this new phase of their relationship. He found ways to make her feel beautiful and desirable, even as her pregnancy progressed, emphasizing their connection beyond physical intimacy.

As the pregnancy progressed, Sira became increasingly aware of the impending changes to their lives. The freedom and spontaneity that defined their early relationship would soon be replaced by the responsibilities and routines of parenthood. The fear of losing that carefree connection played on her mind, creating a quiet anxiety that she shared with Keith during quiet moments. They spent hours discussing their fears, their hopes, and their dreams for their future as a family.

The fear of the unknown loomed large, of course. Parenthood was an uncharted territory, and the anxieties surrounding childbirth, postpartum depression, and the challenges of raising a child were a constant presence in their conversations. They attended parenting classes together, learning about infant care, breastfeeding, and the developmental stages of a newborn. They devoured books and articles, trying to prepare themselves for the realities of parenthood.

Despite the anxieties, a deep sense of love and anticipation permeated their preparations. The nursery, filled with tiny clothes and toys, was a tangible expression of their growing family. The love they shared, once expressed through spontaneous dates and late-night conversations, now found its expression in the careful planning and meticulous preparation for their child's arrival. Their shared experiences, from the initial shock of the pregnancy announcement to the meticulous preparations for their child's arrival, had forged a stronger bond between them, a testament to their commitment and resilience. They were not just a couple, but a team, ready to navigate the challenges of parenthood together. The emotional connection, strengthened by their shared anxieties and joys, was palpable, a silent promise of their unwavering support for each other, a promise they reinforced with each shared glance, each whispered word, and each act of shared preparation for the arrival of their little one.

Planning for the Baby's Arrival

The first tangible step in their baby preparations was the daunting task of choosing a pediatrician. Sira, armed with a meticulously researched list of local pediatricians, complete with online reviews and waiting-room ambiance assessments (a detail Keith found both endearing and slightly alarming), meticulously compared their credentials and philosophies. Keith, initially overwhelmed by the sheer volume of information, found himself surprisingly engaged. He'd always been a practical guy, and the task of ensuring their child had the best possible healthcare became a new kind of challenge, one he relished. They spent hours debating the merits of different practices, comparing insurance coverage, and ultimately settling on a pediatrician whose calm demeanor and holistic approach resonated with both of them. The decision, small in the grand scheme of parenthood, felt like a significant victory, a testament to their ability to work together, even amidst the overwhelming tide of impending parenthood.

Next came the nursery. What started as a simple plan – a gender-neutral room filled with calming pastels – quickly evolved into a full-blown design project. Sira, inspired by Pinterest boards and baby-themed magazines, envisioned a serene space filled with natural light, soft textures, and calming colors. Keith, more pragmatic, focused on functionality and safety. Discussions over paint colors, crib designs, and the optimal placement of changing tables stretched into late nights, filled with laughter and compromise. There were moments of frustration, of course, especially when Sira's vision of a hand-painted mural clashed with Keith's concern about potential lead paint hazards. But these disagreements only served to strengthen their bond, their shared goal of creating a perfect sanctuary for their baby outweighing their individual preferences. The process, however, underscored the stark reality of their limited resources. The perfectly curated nursery, the one that matched their Pinterest dreams, was sadly beyond their reach. They found themselves constantly weighing the need for a beautiful space versus practicality. The hand-painted mural was replaced with a more affordable, equally charming wallpaper. Instead of a high-end crib, they found a sturdy, second-hand one, cleaned and polished to perfection. These compromises, born from necessity, surprisingly enhanced their satisfaction. They understood that creating a nurturing space was about more than just aesthetics; it was about building love and security, and those aspects they could afford in abundance.

The financial strain of pregnancy and preparation became increasingly apparent. Keith's initial exuberance at buying a house quickly gave way to a cautious awareness of their mounting expenses. The cost of prenatal care, baby clothes, diapers, and all the other essentials added up. They both had to work, and Keith's hours increased, leaving less time for them to enjoy each other's company. This constant financial stress became a source of tension, a dark cloud that cast a shadow over their otherwise joyous preparations. Sira, sensitive to Keith's weariness, tried to lighten his load. She took on extra freelance assignments, accepting projects that exhausted her already dwindling energy. Yet, the financial strain remained a constant source of anxiety, leaving them both feeling overwhelmed and stressed. They decided to have a frank discussion, a brutally honest conversation about their finances. Keith admitted his fears, his guilt at not being able to provide Sira with everything she wanted, and his apprehension of the financial burdens of raising a child. Sira, in turn, voiced her own anxieties. She acknowledged her contribution to the financial strain, her own reluctance to spend money on certain items, the constant battles she had within herself to be responsible with the money that they did have. They realized that the weight of their financial burdens wasn't solely Keith's responsibility. They were a team, and tackling their financial uncertainties demanded teamwork.

Navigating the emotional landscape of pregnancy was as challenging as the practical aspects. Sira's mood swings became more pronounced, her anxieties heightened by the constant changes in her body. The once-confident and independent woman found herself grappling with feelings of vulnerability and dependence. Keith, struggling to understand the extent of these hormonal shifts, occasionally misconstrued Sira's reactions, leading to misunderstandings and strained conversations. Their relationship, once a beacon of carefree romance, was now tested by the emotional complexities of pregnancy. To alleviate this, they decided to engage in couples therapy, a decision that initially felt humiliating for both of them. It took a lot of persuasion for Keith, who considered therapy as a sign of weakness, to agree. However, the sessions proved incredibly helpful, offering them a safe space to communicate their feelings and learn to navigate the emotional turbulence. The therapist provided them with tools and strategies to communicate effectively, helping them understand each other's perspectives and alleviate misunderstandings. They learned about healthy communication patterns, conflict resolution techniques, and strategies for managing stress and anxiety. The therapy sessions weren't just about resolving their conflicts; it was about building a stronger foundation for their future as parents.

The prospect of childbirth brought with it a new wave of fear and uncertainty. Sira's anxieties grew, particularly regarding the pain and physical demands of labor. Keith, initially at a loss, attempted to provide comfort and support, often through clumsy attempts at reassurance. He read books about childbirth, trying to educate himself about the process, but his efforts sometimes felt inadequate, leaving Sira feeling more apprehensive. They started attending childbirth classes, a decision that proved beneficial for both of them. The classes provided a structured environment where they could learn about the different stages of labor, pain management techniques, and newborn care. It provided Sira with the practical knowledge and techniques she needed to feel empowered and less afraid. It also gave Keith a more concrete understanding of the process, allowing him to offer more informed support. They practiced breathing exercises together, laughed at the awkward demonstrations, and bonded over the shared experience. These classes not only taught them about childbirth, but strengthened their sense of teamwork and shared responsibility. The knowledge they gained transformed their apprehension into a sense of preparedness, and the shared laughter during the classes eased the tension and created a stronger bond.

In the midst of all the planning and preparations, a significant event occurred – a surprise visit from Noah, Sira's high school ex-boyfriend. The appearance of Noah, unexpected and unwelcome, stirred up unresolved feelings and anxieties. Sira's initial reaction was a mix of surprise and slight discomfort, though she managed to maintain composure and politeness. Keith, observant as always, detected a shift in Sira's demeanor, a subtle tension that wasn't there before. Noah's visit, though seemingly innocuous, threw a wrench into the delicate balance of their preparations. It wasn't a grand romantic gesture, but a simple visit from an old friend, yet it unearthed anxieties and insecurities that they had both managed to keep suppressed during the hectic preparations. The visit served as a reminder of the complexities of their relationship, and the insecurities that still lurked beneath the surface of their seemingly strong bond. Sira's past resurfaced, and Keith's inherent jealousy was rekindled, albeit briefly. They discussed this openly, allowing Keith to verbalize his anxieties and insecurities without blaming Sira. It was a crucial moment of vulnerability and honesty, a step further in their journey to navigate the emotional complexities of their evolving relationship. They discussed Noah's visit, the anxieties it provoked, and the trust they had built. The conversation helped them solidify their commitment, reinforcing the strength of their bond and their dedication to their future together, even amidst the challenges that life had thrown their way. The unexpected visit, instead of jeopardizing their relationship, became a catalyst for deeper understanding and a renewed commitment to face the challenges of their future together. Their path wasn't without its bumps – financial stresses, emotional uncertainties, and unexpected encounters – but their love, fortified by their shared journey, seemed ready to navigate any storm that came their way. The love and anticipation for their child's arrival, palpable in their preparations, remained their constant anchor. Their shared goal of creating a loving and nurturing environment for their child brought them closer, strengthening their bond and setting the stage for a new chapter in their lives. Their journey, though far from perfect, was a testament to the resilience of their love and their unwavering commitment to each other, preparing them for the beautiful chaos of parenthood.

Adjusting to New Roles

The reality of impending parenthood settled upon them like a gentle, yet persistent, snowfall. The initial excitement, the joyous announcement, the whirlwind of doctor's appointments – all of that felt like a distant memory now, replaced by a quiet, contemplative anticipation. Sira, ever the planner, had envisioned a serene transition into motherhood, a peaceful glide into this new chapter. But the reality was more akin to navigating a bustling marketplace – chaotic, slightly overwhelming, but ultimately filled with unexpected joys and discoveries.

Keith, initially hesitant and overwhelmed by the enormity of the change, found himself surprisingly drawn into the meticulous planning. His practical nature, previously directed towards his work and their finances, now channeled into creating a safe and loving haven for their child. He surprised Sira with a beautifully crafted wooden crib, meticulously sanded and stained, a testament to his dedication and burgeoning paternal instincts. The act of creating something tangible for their child, something that represented their shared love and commitment, bridged the gap between his initial apprehension and the growing excitement. It wasn't just a crib; it was a symbol of his evolving role, a tangible expression of his love and commitment.

Their expectations of parenthood were, unsurprisingly, vastly different. Sira, influenced by years of watching her mother effortlessly juggle work, family, and a seemingly endless array of responsibilities, envisioned herself as a supermom. She pictured herself breastfeeding on demand, instantly soothing a crying baby with intuitive knowledge, effortlessly maintaining a pristine home while simultaneously pursuing her career goals. She had compiled countless Pinterest boards filled with meticulously organized nurseries, aesthetically pleasing baby clothes, and perfectly balanced meal plans. This picture, however, started to crumble under the weight of reality.

Keith, on the other hand, had a more grounded, albeit less idealized, vision. He imagined long nights of diaper changes, the chaotic symphony of a crying baby at 3 am, and the constant exhaustion that would undoubtedly accompany the demanding task of parenthood. He anticipated the financial strain, the adjustment to their daily routines, and the inevitable compromises that would be necessary. His expectations weren't romantic; they were realistic. This realism, however, was not devoid of excitement. It was the excitement of facing a challenge together, of rising to the occasion, of forging a new dynamic as a team.

Their differing expectations didn't lead to conflict; instead, it fostered a deeper understanding of each other's perspectives. Sira's meticulous planning, initially perceived by Keith as overly ambitious, began to seem endearing as she expressed anxieties regarding her ability to live up to her own high standards. Keith's pragmatic approach, initially viewed by Sira as lacking in romantic idealism, became a source of comfort and reassurance as she recognized the wisdom in his down-to-earth perspective. They began to meet in the middle, adjusting their expectations to create a shared, realistic, and loving vision of their future family.

The process of purchasing baby items became a surprisingly bonding experience. Choosing a stroller became a heated debate between practicality and aesthetics. Sira's preference for a lightweight, stylish model clashed with Keith's insistence on a sturdy, all-terrain model capable of conquering any sidewalk bump or uneven terrain. Compromise, as always, was the key. They found a stroller that managed to strike a balance between functionality and fashion, a microcosm of their evolving relationship dynamics.

Their conversations evolved beyond logistical planning. They talked about the kind of parents they wanted to be, the values they wanted to instill in their child, the balance between work and family life. Sira's anxieties about the impact of motherhood on her career were met with Keith's unwavering support. He encouraged her to pursue her ambitions while acknowledging the inevitable adjustments required. He promised to shoulder a greater share of the household responsibilities, assuring her that she didn't have to be a supermom to be a loving and capable mother.

Their financial anxieties also came to the forefront. The cost of raising a child was a stark reality that could no longer be ignored. Keith, burdened by the financial responsibilities of their home, found himself working longer hours, taking on additional projects, and meticulously budgeting their expenses. Sira, while hesitant to add to his stress, recognized the importance of contributing financially. She explored part-time work opportunities, balancing the desire to remain professionally engaged with the need to prioritize her health and the baby's well-being.

The prospect of shared parental leave became a source of intense discussion. Sira's initial inclination was to return to work as soon as possible, driven by her ambition and desire to maintain her professional identity. Keith, on the other hand, advocated for an extended period of parental leave, emphasizing the importance of bonding with their child and allowing Sira to recover fully from childbirth. They eventually agreed on a compromise, a period of shared leave that would allow them both to experience the joys and challenges of early parenthood while ensuring that Sira's career wouldn't suffer unduly.

The preparations for the baby's arrival transcended mere logistics; they became a testament to the strength and resilience of their relationship. They learned to navigate their differing expectations, to embrace their individual strengths, and to support each other through the anxieties and challenges that arose. The journey was far from perfect, riddled with minor disagreements and moments of frustration, but their shared commitment to their growing family remained their constant anchor. They weren't just preparing for a baby; they were preparing for a new chapter in their lives, a chapter filled with love, laughter, and the unpredictable joys and challenges of parenthood. Their love, initially tested by insecurities and external pressures, blossomed into a deeper, more profound connection, fortified by the shared experience of creating a life together. The upcoming birth wasn't just about the arrival of a child; it was about the birth of a new family, a family bound together by love, resilience, and the unwavering commitment to face whatever the future may hold. And as they stood on the precipice of this new chapter, holding each other close, they knew that whatever challenges lay ahead, they would face them together, side by side, ready to embrace the beautiful, chaotic adventure that awaited them. Their journey toward parenthood wasn't just a preparation for a baby, it was a testament to the power of their love, and a promise of the beautiful, chaotic journey that awaited them. Their relationship had faced storms, and emerged stronger, ready for the next wave. This next wave, however, was different; it was the wave that would bring them their child, their legacy, their shared future. The shared journey had strengthened their bond, and they faced the future, hand-in-hand, ready to navigate the uncharted waters of parenthood together. Their love, refined by challenges and strengthened by shared experiences, was the cornerstone of their new chapter, a testament to the resilience of their love and a promise of a future filled with family, joy, and unconditional love.

Support System and Family

The first real crack in Sira's curtain of composure appeared during a particularly grueling nesting phase. She'd spent the entire afternoon rearranging the nursery, moving the crib from one corner to another, agonizing over the placement of each tiny onesie. By evening, exhaustion had overtaken her, leaving her slumped on the floor amidst a pile of soft blankets and miniature stuffed animals. Tears welled up, not from sadness, but from the sheer overwhelming pressure of it all. It wasn't just the physical demands of pregnancy; it was the weight of expectation, the fear of failure, and the constant gnawing uncertainty of the future. Keith, sensing her distress, knelt beside her, his touch gentle and reassuring.

"Hey," he whispered, his voice soft as a feather. "What's wrong?"

Sira just shook her head, unable to articulate the jumble of emotions swirling within her. It wasn't a single thing, she realized. It was everything. The fear of childbirth, the financial anxieties, the lingering insecurities about their relationship, the uncertainty of balancing parenthood with her career aspirations – it all threatened to suffocate her.

"It's... it's all too much," she finally managed, her voice choked with emotion.

Keith gathered her into his arms, holding her close as she finally let the tears flow freely. He didn't try to fix it, not immediately. He just held her, letting her release the pent-up tension and fear. That night, as they lay in bed, he gently suggested they reach out to their families. The idea had been simmering in the back of his mind, a quiet recognition that they couldn't, and shouldn't, face this alone.

The next day, Sira called her mother. The conversation started hesitantly, with cautious words and carefully chosen phrases. But as Sira poured out her anxieties, her mother's voice, usually filled with a cheerful energy, softened with understanding and empathy. She reassured Sira that she wasn't alone, that this was a journey shared by countless mothers before her. She offered practical advice, sharing her own experiences, and even volunteered to come and help prepare the nursery.

Meanwhile, Keith reached out to his parents. Their reaction was different, more subdued, but no less supportive. His father, a man of few words, simply said, "We're here for you, son. Whatever you need." His mother, however, was a whirlwind of activity. She started making calls, arranging for help with household chores, and even offered to cook meals for them once the baby arrived.

The support from their families wasn't just practical; it was emotional. It was the knowledge that they weren't alone in this journey, that there was a network of love and support surrounding them, ready to catch them if they stumbled. Sira's best friend, Maya, also stepped up, offering to help with anything from grocery shopping to running errands. She even organized a baby shower, a joyous celebration filled with laughter, tears, and the comforting warmth of friendship.

The impact of this support system was profound. It alleviated some of the pressure Sira felt, allowing her to focus on the joy of expecting a child without being completely overwhelmed by the challenges. The constant stream of help allowed Keith to dedicate more time to Sira, bolstering their relationship and strengthening their bond as they prepared for the arrival of their child. He learned to articulate his support more effectively, actively listening to Sira's concerns and offering practical solutions, rather than trying to minimize her anxieties.

Their families also played a vital role in navigating some of the more challenging aspects of their relationship. Sira's initial insecurities about Keith's ex-girlfriends, which had previously caused significant tension, began to fade as she saw how supportive his family was towards her. They welcomed her into their fold, treating her not just as their future daughter-in-law, but as a cherished member of their family. This acceptance helped bridge the gap between her and Keith's past relationships, reducing the sense of competition and rivalry that had plagued their early days.

Similarly, Keith's family's presence helped ease some of the tensions surrounding his past financial struggles. His parents offered practical financial assistance, making it easier to manage the expenses associated with the impending arrival of their child. They understood the pressure Keith had faced and didn't judge his past mistakes. Their support didn't come with conditions or criticisms; it was a silent act of faith in their son and his evolving relationship with Sira.

The support wasn't always smooth sailing. There were moments of tension, of disagreements about parenting styles and childcare philosophies. Keith's mother, for instance, had a firm traditional outlook that sometimes clashed with Sira's more modern ideas. But these disagreements were approached with understanding and compromise. They learned to navigate their differences, respecting each other's perspectives and finding common ground.

Sira's own relationship with her mother wasn't without its challenges. Her mother, despite her unwavering support, occasionally voiced concerns about Sira's career ambitions and her ability to balance work and motherhood. Sira, however, found her mother's anxieties stemmed from a place of love and concern, not judgment. They worked through these differences, finding a balance that respected both Sira's independence and her mother's protective instincts.

Keith's relationship with his father continued to be characterized by quiet support and practical help. He wasn't a man of lavish displays of affection, but his actions spoke louder than words. He helped Keith with repairs around the house, assisted with the nursery setup, and quietly provided financial assistance whenever needed, ensuring a sense of security for Keith and Sira. It was an unspoken understanding between father and son, a testament to the enduring bond forged over years.

The arrival of their child changed everything, and yet, it changed nothing. The chaotic energy of their previous lives softened, replaced by a profound sense of purpose and unity. They weren't simply a couple navigating the challenges of adulthood; they were a family, a team, working together to raise a child amidst the beautiful chaos of life. Their support system wasn't merely a network of assistance; it was a foundation, a bedrock of love and support that helped them weather the storms and navigate the unexpected turns in their journey. Their relationship, once tested by insecurities and external pressures, had transformed into something stronger, more resilient, and undeniably more profound. The combined support from both families had not only facilitated the practical preparations for the baby's arrival but had also healed old wounds, strengthening their bond as a couple and creating a strong foundation for their new family. It was a testament to the power of family, friendship, and the unwavering support that enabled them to face the future with confidence and unwavering love. The support network wasn't just a safety net; it was an integral part of their journey towards parenthood, a constant reminder that they were surrounded by love and that they were not alone. The unwavering support of their families and friends had become an indispensable part of their story, a testament to the strength of their bonds and the power of community in the face of life's greatest challenges. Their journey, initially fraught with anxieties and uncertainties, blossomed into a beautiful tapestry woven with threads of love, support, and the unwavering commitment to their family. The birth of their child was not just the beginning of a new chapter, but a testament to the power of unity and the enduring strength of the bonds they had carefully cultivated.

Growing Closer Through Shared Experience

The exhaustion that followed the nursery rearrangement wasn't just physical; it was emotional. Sira felt the weight of expectations pressing down on her, a silent pressure cooker threatening to burst. She worried about being a good mother, about providing for her child, about the potential for failure looming large in her mind. These anxieties, once simmering beneath the surface, now bubbled to the forefront, threatening to overwhelm her.

Keith, ever observant, noticed the shift in Sira's demeanor. He didn't dismiss her fears as irrational; instead, he met them head-on, acknowledging the validity of her concerns. He listened patiently as she confessed her anxieties, her voice trembling slightly with unshed tears. It wasn't a casual conversation; it was a vulnerable sharing, a peeling back of layers that had been carefully constructed to mask her insecurities.

"It's okay to feel overwhelmed, Sira," he said softly, his voice a soothing balm against her fears. "It's a huge change, a massive undertaking. We're in this together, and we'll figure it out, step by step."

His words, simple yet profound, provided a sense of calm that she desperately needed. He didn't offer solutions, not yet. He simply offered his presence, his unwavering support, a silent reassurance that she wasn't alone in navigating this challenging terrain.

The following days were a blur of activity, a whirlwind of preparations for the baby's arrival. They painted the nursery, assembling the crib with a mixture of excitement and clumsy fumbling. They washed tiny clothes, each garment a tangible symbol of the life growing within Sira. These mundane tasks, initially daunting, became moments of shared intimacy, a silent conversation woven into the fabric of their daily lives.

One evening, while sorting through a mountain of baby clothes, Sira found herself laughing at Keith's attempts to fold a tiny onesie. His concentration was so intense, his brow furrowed in concentration, that it was impossible not to be charmed by his clumsiness. It was a small moment, a fleeting instance of shared laughter, yet it held a profound significance. It was a testament to the growing bond between them, a silent acknowledgement of their shared journey into parenthood.

The shared experience of assembling the baby's crib was another pivotal moment. They struggled with the instructions, their frustration momentarily flaring before melting into shared laughter as they wrestled with stubborn screws and confusing diagrams. It was a bonding experience, a reminder that they were a team, navigating the challenges of parenthood together. The clumsiness, the frustration, the eventual triumph of assembling the crib – it all contributed to a deeper sense of connection, a shared experience that transcended the mere act of putting together furniture.

As the weeks progressed, their conversations evolved. They weren't just discussing practicalities; they were delving into deeper emotional territory. Sira confessed her fears about childbirth, the pain, the unknown. Keith, initially hesitant to fully engage with these anxieties, found himself drawn into the intimacy of her vulnerability. He listened, offering reassurance and empathy, his words carefully chosen to comfort and support her. He learned to recognize the subtle nuances of her emotional state, the subtle shifts in her demeanor that signaled her anxieties.

Their conversations extended beyond the practical aspects of pregnancy. They discussed their hopes and dreams for their child, their fears and insecurities about the future. They shared their vulnerabilities, their hopes, their anxieties, creating a space for honest and open communication. The conversations weren't always easy;

sometimes, disagreements arose, disagreements that were resolved not through arguments but through mutual understanding and compromise.

One evening, amidst the flurry of preparations, they sat on the porch, sipping tea as the setting sun cast long shadows across their lawn. Sira rested her head on Keith's shoulder, the weight of her pregnancy a palpable presence. The silence between them wasn't awkward; it was comfortable, a quiet understanding that transcended words. It was in these moments of shared stillness, of quiet contemplation, that their bond deepened, strengthened by their shared journey into parenthood.

The presence of Keith's ex-girlfriends, a source of tension earlier in their relationship, faded into the background. The impending arrival of their child shifted the focus, creating a common ground that overshadowed past insecurities. Sira realized that Keith's relationships with his exes were, in fact, friendly and devoid of romantic intentions. Seeing his genuine excitement about fatherhood, his dedication to their shared future, eased her fears significantly.

The support of both their families became invaluable during this period. Sira's parents, initially hesitant about their daughter's relationship, embraced their future grandchild with open arms, their anxieties about Sira's relationship with Keith melting away as they witnessed their growing commitment. Keith's parents, too, were thrilled at the prospect of becoming grandparents. Their involvement wasn't merely about helping with preparations; it was a gesture of acceptance, a silent affirmation of their support for the couple's journey.

Family dinners, once tense affairs, now became occasions of shared laughter and lighthearted banter. The shared experience of preparing for the baby's arrival broke down barriers, forging a stronger bond between Sira, Keith, and their families. The presence of their supportive families played a huge role in easing anxieties and creating a secure environment to welcome their little one. It was during these gatherings that Sira realized how much Keith valued family and how eager he was to welcome this new member into their lives.

The unexpected visit from Sira's high school ex-boyfriend, a potential source of conflict, was handled with grace and maturity. Keith's reaction was not one of jealousy or possessiveness, but of calm understanding. He saw Sira's interaction with her ex as a friendly encounter, not a threat to their relationship. This display of trust and confidence further solidified Sira's feelings for Keith.

As the due date approached, Sira and Keith found themselves deeply intertwined, their lives irrevocably bound by the shared experience of preparing for parenthood. The challenges they had faced, the insecurities they had overcome, had only served to strengthen their bond. They were not just a couple; they were a team, a family in the making, ready to welcome their child into a world filled with love, support, and the unwavering commitment of two souls bound together by a shared journey. The anxieties remained, but they were now tempered by the confidence born from their shared experiences and the unwavering support of their loved ones. Their love story was no longer just a college romance; it was a testament to the resilience of love, the strength of their bond, and the beautiful chaos of building a life together. The pregnancy, initially a source of tension and uncertainty, had become a catalyst for their growth, a transformative experience that had deepened their connection and prepared them for the profound journey of parenthood. The preparations for the baby's arrival had not only created a cozy and loving home but had also laid the foundation for a strong and lasting family. Their love story, once fraught with challenges, was now evolving into something even more beautiful, more resilient, and more deeply fulfilling.

Chapter 7:

Labor and Delivery

The air in the delivery room hung thick with anticipation, a stark contrast to the rhythmic whoosh of the heart rate monitor beside Sira's bed. Sweat beaded on her forehead, mirroring the glistening droplets on Keith's brow as he gripped her hand, his knuckles bone-white. The pain, a relentless wave crashing against the shores of her body, stole her breath, leaving her gasping for air between contractions. Each surge was a brutal reminder of the monumental task ahead, a test of her physical and emotional strength. She'd envisioned this moment countless times, a beautiful, serene arrival of their child. The reality was far grittier, far more primal.

Keith, usually so composed and quick-witted, was a whirlwind of nervous energy. He paced the small confines of the room, occasionally stopping to whisper words of encouragement, his voice trembling slightly. He'd been a rock throughout her pregnancy, patiently attending doctor's appointments, soothing her anxieties, and even attempting—with varying degrees of success—to navigate the complexities of nesting and preparing for parenthood. Now, though, his usual confidence seemed to have evaporated, replaced by a palpable anxiety that mirrored her own.

The nurses, seasoned veterans of countless births, moved with a quiet efficiency, their actions a soothing counterpoint to Sira's escalating pain. They monitored her progress, offering words of comfort and support, a gentle presence in the storm. One, a kind woman with warm eyes and a gentle smile, offered Sira a cool cloth to wipe her face, her touch reassuring and calming. Another quietly adjusted the pillows, making her as comfortable as possible given the circumstances. Their expertise and care were a lifeline in the chaotic landscape of labor.

The contractions intensified, each one a more ferocious assault than the last. Sira's breath hitched, her body arching, her screams muffled by Keith's hand pressed against her mouth, a mixture of pain and exertion escaping in guttural moans. She dug her fingers into his hand, her grip tenacious, clinging to him as if her life depended on it. And in a way, it did. He was her anchor, her strength, her unwavering support in the eye of this emotional hurricane.

Between contractions, brief moments of respite offered glimmers of hope. The exhaustion was profound, a bone-deep weariness that threatened to consume her, but the promise of meeting their child pushed her onward. Keith's presence, his unwavering support, his whispered words of encouragement, kept her going when she felt like giving up. She clung to his words, to the strength she found in his touch, to the love that connected them in this profound, shared experience.

The doctor arrived, her presence authoritative yet comforting. She examined Sira, her assessment calm and professional, her words measured and reassuring. Sira, in a moment of clarity between contractions, understood that the final push was near. A surge of adrenaline, a mixture of fear and exhilaration, coursed through her veins. She braced herself, focusing on her breath, on Keith's hand in hers, on the promise of new beginnings.

The final contractions were a blur, a symphony of pain and exertion. Sira pushed with every ounce of her being, her body straining, her muscles burning. Keith chanted words of encouragement, his voice a steady rhythm amidst the chaos, a beacon of hope in the storm. The nurses guided her, their hands firm yet gentle, their words a calming balm.

Then, a gasp. A cry. A tiny, perfect sound that echoed in the room, a symbol of life's resilience, a testament to the power of love and perseverance. Sira's baby had arrived. A wave of relief, so potent it almost knocked her off her feet, washed over her. The pain receded, replaced by an overwhelming surge of love, so profound and all-consuming it left her breathless.

The nurses gently placed the baby on Sira's chest, skin to skin. The tiny body, so warm and soft, nestled against her, a silent promise of a future filled with love and adventure. Sira looked down at her child, her heart overflowing with an emotion she couldn't quite articulate. It was a love so intense, so pure, it brought tears to her eyes. It was a love that transcended the pain, the exhaustion, the anxieties of the past months. This was the culmination of their journey, the reward for their perseverance, the beginning of a new chapter.

Keith, tears streaming down his face, leaned in, his gaze fixed on their child. His hand gently brushed against the baby's cheek, a tender touch that spoke volumes. He whispered words of love and welcome, his voice thick with emotion. He was a father. They were parents. And in that moment, amidst the chaos and exhaustion, they were utterly, completely, irrevocably in love.

The first few hours were a haze of blurry images and intense emotions. The nurses helped Sira and Keith navigate the initial challenges of newborn care. They showed them how to swaddle the baby, how to burp them, how to change a diaper. Their instructions were patient and clear, their support unwavering. The couple, still reeling from the intensity of the birth, were clumsy and hesitant at first, but they learned quickly, working together, their movements synchronized by the common goal of caring for their newborn child.

As the initial shock began to wear off, the reality of their new situation began to sink in. They were parents. Their lives had irrevocably changed, forever altered by the arrival of this tiny human being. The sleepless nights, the constant demands, the overwhelming responsibility – they were all part of this new reality, a reality they were ready to embrace. They were tired, exhausted, but filled with a love so profound and all-consuming it fueled their determination to face whatever challenges lay ahead.

The first few days were a blur of feeding, changing, and cuddling. Sira struggled with breastfeeding, experiencing the common difficulties that many new mothers face. Keith offered unwavering support, helping with night feeds, soothing the baby, and making sure Sira was as comfortable as possible. He learned how to change a diaper with remarkable speed, mastering the art of soothing a crying infant with surprising ease. He had surprised himself with his innate nurturing instincts.

Their relationship, already tested by the anxieties of pregnancy and their past struggles, was now further challenged by the demands of parenthood. Sleep deprivation took its toll, causing friction and misunderstandings. The constant attention needed by the baby made it difficult for them to connect as a couple, to recapture the intimacy they once enjoyed. Yet, amidst the exhaustion, a new kind of connection blossomed, a shared responsibility, a common goal that strengthened their bond in ways they hadn't anticipated. Their love, once fragile and uncertain, had grown stronger, more resilient, tempered by the crucible of parenthood.

The shift in dynamics was profound. Keith, initially hesitant and uncertain about his role as a father, discovered an untapped well of patience and tenderness. He was utterly devoted to his child, his love as powerful and protective as any instinctual drive. Sira, overwhelmed at times by the physical and emotional demands of motherhood, found strength in Keith's unwavering support, his capacity for love exceeding even her highest expectations. Their roles as individuals were altered, their identities molded and transformed by this new chapter of their lives. They were parents, and nothing would ever be quite the same. But as they looked at their sleeping baby, nestled securely in their arms, they knew that this new reality, this new beginning, was a journey they were ready to face together. The challenges remained, but their love, forged in the fires of adversity, was stronger than ever. They were ready for whatever came next.

Welcoming the Baby

The doctor's voice, a low murmur previously lost in the symphony of Sira's pain, cut through the tension. "It's a girl," he announced, his tone laced with a quiet reverence that mirrored the awe settling over the room. A wave of relief, so profound it almost buckled her knees, washed over Sira. The pain, still present but somehow less ferocious, receded into the background, replaced by an overwhelming surge of pure, unadulterated joy. Tears streamed down her face, a mixture of exhaustion and elation, as she gazed at the tiny, perfect being cradled in the nurse's arms.

Keith, his face etched with a mixture of exhaustion and wonder, knelt beside the bed, his eyes fixed on their daughter. He reached out a trembling hand, his touch hesitant, reverent, as if afraid to break the fragile magic of the moment. The nurse gently placed the baby in his arms, and a hush fell over the room. The world seemed to hold its breath, suspended in the delicate balance of this new life.

Their daughter, with her tiny fingers curled around Keith's thumb, her eyes closed in peaceful slumber, was breathtakingly beautiful. Her skin, soft as silk, was the color of fresh cream, her dark lashes resting against cheekbones already hinting at the delicate structure of her face. A wisp of dark hair, the same shade as Sira's, lay nestled against her forehead. She was perfect, a miniature masterpiece of nature's artistry.

The initial shock of seeing her gave way to an overwhelming rush of love, a tidal wave of emotion that swept over both Keith and Sira, binding them together in a connection far deeper than anything they had experienced before. This was it, the culmination of months of anticipation, fear, and overwhelming change. This tiny human being was the tangible embodiment of their love, their shared journey, their future.

The next few hours blurred into a hazy montage of joyous chaos. The nurses fussed over the baby, weighing her, measuring her, and marveling at her perfection. Keith, still holding her close, whispered words of love and reassurance, his voice thick with emotion. Sira, despite the lingering aches in her body, felt an incredible sense of peace. The exhaustion was present, but it was overshadowed by the profound joy radiating from her heart.

The first feeding was a tentative, clumsy affair, a delicate dance between instinct and inexperience. Sira, guided by the nurses, managed to latch their daughter, a moment of tender intimacy that solidified the bond between mother and child. The baby's tiny suckling, a soft rhythmic sound, filled the room with a sense of contentment.

As the initial euphoria subsided, the weight of their new reality settled upon them. The challenges of parenthood, the sleepless nights, the constant demands of a tiny human being—all these were still to come. But facing them together, hand in hand, felt different now. They were no longer just Keith and Sira; they were a family.

The trip home was a slow, deliberate process. Keith drove cautiously, his eyes constantly darting to the infant car seat in the back, ensuring his precious cargo was safe and secure. Sira, nestled beside him, held her daughter's hand, a small, fragile connection that felt immensely powerful. The world outside seemed to fade, replaced by the soft rhythmic breathing of their child, a lullaby to their new beginning.

The house, once a symbol of their struggles and anxieties, now felt different. It was filled with a new energy, a vibrant, life-affirming pulse that permeated every room. The nursery, carefully prepared with months of meticulous planning, felt less like a room and more like a sanctuary, a haven for their precious daughter.

The first few weeks were a whirlwind of sleep deprivation, diaper changes, and endless feedings. Keith, surprised by his own aptitude for this new role, discovered a hidden wellspring of patience and tenderness. His initial reservations about fatherhood had completely vanished, replaced by an overwhelming love for his daughter and a deep-seated commitment to Sira.

Sira, too, underwent a transformation. The anxieties and insecurities that had plagued her throughout her pregnancy seemed to melt away in the face of motherhood. The overwhelming love for her child gave her a strength she hadn't known she possessed. The constant demands of motherhood tested her limits, but they also revealed a resilience she never imagined.

Their relationship, already tested by countless obstacles, emerged stronger and more profound. The petty arguments, the insecurities, the lingering shadows of past relationships—all of these seemed insignificant in the face of their shared joy and the responsibility of parenthood. They faced each challenge, each sleepless night, each moment of doubt, together. Their love was no longer just a romantic connection; it had become a partnership, a foundation upon which their family was built.

As the weeks turned into months, their daughter blossomed. Her smiles, once rare and fleeting, became frequent and infectious. Her laughter, a tinkling melody, filled their home with joy and warmth. They watched her grow, each milestone celebrated with a mixture of pride and wonder. They were parents, yes, but they were also best friends, lovers, partners. Their journey was far from over, but with each new challenge, their love grew stronger. They were ready to face the future, together, as a family.

The presence of Keith's ex-girlfriends, once a source of conflict, became less of a concern. They understood that their relationship was different now, matured by the responsibility of parenthood. The friendly contact remained, but the underlying tension had dissipated, replaced by a mutual respect and understanding.

Even the surprise visit from Sira's high school ex-boyfriend, which had once seemed like a significant threat, was handled with a newfound maturity and confidence. Sira, stronger and more secure in herself and her relationship with Keith, was able to navigate the encounter with grace and composure.

Their journey hadn't been easy. The financial struggles, the anxieties surrounding the pregnancy, the challenges of their relationship—all these had tested them to their limits. But through it all, they had found their way back to each other, their love reinforced and redefined by the arrival of their daughter.

The birth of their child marked not just the beginning of a new chapter in their lives, but the culmination of their journey. It was a testament to their resilience, their capacity for love, and their unwavering commitment to each other. The future was still uncertain, filled with new challenges and unforeseen obstacles. But as they gazed at their sleeping daughter, nestled securely in their arms, Keith and Sira knew they were ready. They were a family, and together, they would face whatever life threw their way. Their love story, once marked by uncertainty and doubt, had found its happy ending, not as a destination but as a journey that would continue to unfold, chapter by chapter, filled with love, laughter, and the endless adventures of parenthood. The challenges would continue, perhaps even intensify, but they were ready. They were a family, and that was all that mattered.

The First Few Days

The first night was a blur. The sterile scent of the hospital was replaced by the sweet, milky smell of their daughter, Maya. Sira, exhausted beyond measure, drifted in and out of sleep, her hand instinctively reaching for the tiny form nestled against her chest. The rhythmic rise and fall of Maya's breath was a soothing lullaby, a stark contrast to the cacophony of pain that had filled the previous day. Keith, equally sleep-deprived, watched over them both, his face etched with a mixture of awe and apprehension. He'd held babies before – nieces, nephews – but holding his baby, his daughter, felt profoundly different. It was a weight of responsibility, a profound connection that transcended the simple act of holding a small human. He felt a surge of protective instinct so strong it almost hurt.

The hospital staff, efficient and kind, provided a crash course in newborn care. They demonstrated how to swaddle Maya, how to burp her, how to change her diaper – a process that seemed both ridiculously simple and terrifyingly complex simultaneously. Sira, her body still sore, struggled to master the art of breastfeeding, battling cracked nipples and a persistent feeling of inadequacy. Keith, meanwhile, learned to soothe Maya's cries with gentle rocking and soft humming. He discovered a surprising talent for burping her, a skill he hadn't known he possessed. The tiny, helpless creature in his arms seemed to respond to his touch, her tiny fingers wrapping around his.

Leaving the hospital two days later felt both exhilarating and terrifying. The controlled environment of the birthing suite was exchanged for the chaos of their own home, a home suddenly far too quiet without the constant hum of hospital equipment. The reality of parenthood slammed into them with the force of a tidal wave. Sleep became a luxury, a fragmented, precious commodity snatched in short bursts between feedings, diaper changes, and the endless cycle of soothing a crying baby. The first few nights were a blur of bleary-eyed exhaustion, punctuated by moments of pure, overwhelming joy. The simple act of watching Maya sleep, her tiny chest rising and falling, filled Sira and Keith with a love so profound it bordered on the spiritual.

The practicalities of newborn life quickly overwhelmed them. The seemingly endless supply of diapers, the constant laundry, the sheer volume of tiny clothes – it was all a sensory overload. Sira, still recovering from childbirth, found herself overwhelmed by the sheer amount of work involved. Keith, bless his heart, tried his best, but his inexperience often left him feeling helpless and frustrated. There were moments of tension, brief flare-ups of exhaustion-fueled frustration. One particularly brutal morning, after a night of Maya's relentless crying, Sira snapped, her exhaustion blurring the line between maternal instinct and irritable outburst. Keith, sensing her frustration, pulled her close. He didn't try to offer solutions; he just held her, his embrace a silent apology for his own fumbling efforts.

"I'm sorry," he whispered, his voice thick with sleeplessness. "I don't know what I'm doing."

Sira, tears streaming down her face, buried her head in his chest. "Neither do I," she admitted, her voice trembling. "But we'll figure it out. Together."

And they did. Slowly, gradually, they found a rhythm, a balance between their own needs and the demands of their newborn daughter. Keith learned to anticipate Maya's needs, recognizing the subtle cues that signaled hunger or discomfort. Sira, despite her physical limitations, found a newfound strength, a resilience she hadn't known she possessed. They discovered a quiet intimacy in the shared exhaustion, the unspoken understanding that passed between them in the dead of night. Their love, once tested by doubt and insecurity, grew stronger, deepened by the shared experience of parenthood.

Visits from family and friends were a mixed blessing. Well-meaning relatives showered them with gifts and advice, much of it unsolicited and occasionally conflicting. Sira's mother, ever practical, provided invaluable help with the household chores, allowing Sira to focus on bonding with Maya. Keith's friends, initially hesitant, slowly adapted to the new reality, their visits less focused on socializing and more on lending a hand, whether it was picking up groceries or offering to hold Maya while Sira took a much-needed shower.

The financial strain remained. Keith, juggling his job and the demands of fatherhood, felt the pressure mounting. They had to make adjustments – cut back on expenses, rely on help from family. The dream of the perfect nursery, painstakingly planned before Maya's arrival, remained largely unrealized, replaced by a makeshift arrangement in their bedroom. But they learned to prioritize, to focus on what truly mattered – their love for each other and their love for Maya.

The first few weeks were challenging. There were nights when Sira felt overwhelmed, questioning her abilities, battling the postpartum blues. Keith, though initially flustered by the lack of a clear instruction manual on parenting, became a dedicated father, learning to navigate the emotional minefield of infancy with a blend of patience, empathy, and a growing confidence. He learned to anticipate Maya's needs, recognizing subtle cues – a whimper that meant hunger, a grimace indicating discomfort. He discovered a patience he never knew he possessed, soothing her cries with a gentle rocking motion that became their ritual.

One particularly difficult evening, after Maya had cried relentlessly for hours, Sira collapsed onto the bed, tears streaming down her face. The sheer exhaustion had shattered her composure, leaving her feeling utterly inadequate. Keith, seeing her distress, didn't offer platitudes or empty reassurances. He simply sat beside her, pulling her close, and held her until her sobs subsided.

"It's okay," he whispered, his voice hoarse with fatigue. "We're in this together."

His words, simple yet profound, were more comforting than any grand declaration of love. They were a testament to their bond, a recognition of their shared struggles and triumphs.

The presence of Keith's ex-girlfriends remained a subtle but persistent tension. They were supportive, sending gifts and offering words of encouragement, but Sira still felt a pang of insecurity whenever Keith spoke to them. She tried to dismiss her feelings as irrational jealousy, but the constant reminders of his past relationships lingered, creating a subtle unease in her heart. She found herself confiding in her therapist again, this time about her anxieties about balancing her own needs and desires with the demands of motherhood and a relationship still navigating its own complexities. She had anticipated the challenges of motherhood, but not how it would impact her existing relationship.

The arrival of Maya had undeniably changed their dynamic. Their once vibrant social life was now punctuated by late nights, early mornings, and the ever-present demand for attention from their tiny daughter. They still found moments of intimacy, stolen glimpses of connection amidst the chaos of diaper changes and feedings, but the spontaneous outings and carefree laughter were replaced by a more deliberate, more deeply entrenched form of love – a quiet, unwavering commitment forged in the crucible of shared responsibility.

And as they navigated the sleepless nights and endless demands of newborn life, Sira and Keith began to see their relationship not as a romantic fairytale, but as a real, imperfect, profoundly rewarding partnership. It wasn't perfect, and it would continue to be tested, but amidst the chaos and uncertainty of early parenthood, their love had found a new and stronger foundation – a foundation built on shared experiences, mutual respect, and the unwavering bond of a family. The journey continued, each day a new challenge, each night a victory in survival. But they faced it together, hand-in-hand, their love strengthened by the miracle they had created. They had survived the first few days, and somehow, that felt like a momentous achievement. The future was unwritten, but as they gazed at their sleeping daughter, they knew, with a certainty that went beyond words, that they could face anything together.

Adjusting to Parenthood

The first few weeks were a chaotic blur of feeding schedules, diaper changes, and the constant, low-level hum of exhaustion. Sira, who had envisioned a serene postpartum experience filled with gentle rocking and bonding moments, found herself grappling with the harsh realities of sleep deprivation and the relentless demands of a newborn. The idyllic images she'd crafted in her mind were quickly replaced by the gritty truth of spit-up, leaky breasts, and the persistent, piercing cry that echoed through their once-quiet home. Keith, despite his initial apprehension, proved to be a surprisingly adept father. He embraced the messy reality of parenthood with a willingness to learn and a patience that Sira hadn't anticipated. He changed diapers, burped Maya with surprising expertise, and even managed to master the art of soothing her frantic cries with a gentle rocking motion.

Their relationship, already tested by external pressures, underwent a profound transformation. The romantic dinners and leisurely weekend getaways were replaced by hurried meals eaten in shifts, and the stolen kisses were now fleeting moments snatched between feeding sessions. Sira, fueled by hormones and exhaustion, was prone to emotional outbursts, her insecurities magnified by the monumental shift in her life. Keith, struggling to balance the demands of his job with the needs of his family, found himself feeling overwhelmed and frustrated. There were moments of intense friction, arguments erupting over seemingly insignificant issues – the temperature of the baby's bath water, the best brand of diapers, the proper way to swaddle a newborn. These arguments, however, were interspersed with moments of profound tenderness, shared smiles, and a deep sense of unity born from their shared experience.

One particularly challenging evening, Sira found herself sobbing uncontrollably, overwhelmed by the sheer weight of her responsibilities. Keith, sensing her distress, gently gathered her in his arms, his touch a soothing balm against the storm raging within her. He listened patiently as she poured out her frustrations, her fears, and her anxieties – anxieties that went beyond the typical anxieties of a new mother. The pressure of managing their finances, the lingering insecurities about Keith's relationships with his exes, the weight of her own past traumas – all of it converged into a tidal wave of emotion that threatened to engulf her.

Keith, for the first time, truly understood the depth of Sira's struggles. He hadn't fully grasped the scope of her experience before, dismissing some of her concerns as postpartum hormones or emotional manipulation. He now recognized that her anxieties stemmed from a complex interplay of factors, and his initial assumptions had been unfair and dismissive. He held her close, whispering words of comfort and reassurance, acknowledging the immense challenges they were facing. That night, a crucial shift occurred in their dynamic. They moved beyond a transactional relationship – one defined by the pressures of their past – to something deeper, a partnership forged in the crucible of shared struggle. They started to communicate with a newfound honesty and vulnerability, sharing their fears, their doubts, and their hopes for the future.

Their therapist, Dr. Anya Sharma, had provided them with invaluable tools for navigating the complexities of their relationship and the stresses of parenthood. She helped them establish healthy communication patterns, teaching them how to express their needs and concerns without resorting to blame or accusation. She also helped Sira address her underlying anxieties, providing her with coping mechanisms and strategies for managing her emotional responses. The therapy sessions weren't a magic cure, but they provided a safe space for them to confront their challenges and build a stronger, more resilient foundation for their relationship.

The transition into parenthood wasn't just about adapting to the demands of a newborn; it was a profound transformation of their individual identities and their relationship as a couple. Sira, once a vibrant, independent young woman, found herself surrendering to the demands of motherhood, a surrender that wasn't always easy. Her sense of self shifted, as she became defined not just by her aspirations and dreams but also by her role as a mother. Keith, too, underwent a significant change. He became more responsible, more mature, more grounded in his sense of purpose. He discovered a depth of love and protectiveness that he never knew he possessed.

The mundane tasks of parenthood – the endless laundry, the sleepless nights, the constant cycle of feeding and changing – became a tapestry of shared experiences, a bonding ritual that solidified their connection. The simple act of sharing a tired smile across a room, the silent understanding exchanged during a 3 am feeding session, the shared burden of exhaustion – these became the building blocks of a new kind of intimacy, one forged not in romantic gestures but in the shared reality of parenthood.

Maya, their daughter, became the center of their world, a tiny human being who brought immense joy into their lives, even as she challenged them in ways they never imagined. Her laughter, her smiles, her tiny grasp on their fingers – these small moments held an immense power, capable of erasing the fatigue and dissolving the anxieties that had plagued them. Their shared love for Maya became the unifying force that bound them together, deepening their connection beyond the romantic entanglement of their college days.

The financial pressures didn't dissipate overnight. The cost of raising a child, the mortgage payments, the everyday expenses – they all weighed heavily on them. Keith continued to work tirelessly, taking on extra shifts and freelance projects to provide for their growing family. Sira, once ambitious about pursuing her career, found herself putting her own aspirations on hold, focusing on the immediate needs of their daughter. They had moments of resentment, of frustration, of questioning the sacrifices they were making. But these moments were always outweighed by the unwavering commitment they had towards each other and their child. They learned to budget carefully, to prioritize, to seek assistance when needed. They discovered a strength in their shared struggle, a resilience born from their mutual support.

The presence of Keith's ex-girlfriends remained a source of tension, though it became less pronounced as Sira began to see their relationships from a different perspective. She realized that Keith's friendships with his exes didn't diminish his love for her; they were simply a part of his past, a past that she couldn't erase, but one she could learn to accept. The insecurities still lingered, but they were no longer as overwhelming, as the profound love and commitment shared with Keith for their daughter overshadowed the past.

The unexpected visit from Sira's high school ex-boyfriend served as a reminder of the paths not taken, the choices made, and the life they were building together. It was a moment of introspection, a reflection on the journey they had undertaken and the challenges they had overcome. The past had shaped them, but it no longer dictated their future. They had chosen each other, a choice that had been solidified and deepened by the incredible journey of parenthood.

As the months passed, their lives began to settle into a new rhythm, a rhythm dictated by Maya's milestones, her first smiles, her first steps, her first words. The chaos persisted, but it was a manageable chaos, a chaos they navigated hand-in-hand, their love a sturdy ship weathering the storms of parenthood. Their relationship evolved, transforming from a passionate college romance into a mature, steadfast partnership, a partnership defined by shared responsibility, unwavering commitment, and the unwavering love they held for their daughter, Maya, the tiny human who had irrevocably changed their lives and brought them together in a way they never anticipated. The future remained uncertain, filled with unforeseen challenges and opportunities. But as they looked at their sleeping daughter, nestled securely in her crib, Keith and

Sira knew, with a certainty that settled deep within their hearts, that they were ready to face whatever came their way, together. Their journey was far from over, but amidst the exhaustion and the chaos, they had found something profound, something enduring, something truly beautiful. They had found their family, and in that discovery, they had found a love that was stronger, deeper, and more resilient than they ever imagined possible.

Shifting Dynamics

The first few months were a blur, a whirlwind of sleep deprivation and the constant, insistent demands of a tiny human. Sira, remembering her romanticized notions of motherhood, chuckled ruefully. The reality was far messier, far more demanding, and far less picturesque than the serene images she'd conjured in her mind. The gentle rocking and bonding moments were interspersed with frantic searches for lost pacifiers, midnight feedings that stretched into dawn, and the ever-present anxiety of wondering if she was doing everything right.

Keith, however, surprised even himself. He hadn't anticipated the depth of his paternal instincts, the overwhelming surge of love that washed over him every time he gazed at his daughter, Maya. He wasn't just a boyfriend anymore; he was a father, a provider, a protector. He learned to change diapers with surprising dexterity, mastered the art of burping a baby without launching projectile vomit across the room, and even developed a knack for soothing Maya's cries with a gentle humming that seemed to magically quiet her distress.

Their relationship shifted, subtly at first, then with increasing clarity. The passionate, often tumultuous romance of their college years evolved into something deeper, more profound, more resilient. It wasn't just about stolen kisses and late-night talks anymore; it was about shared responsibility, unwavering commitment, and the unbreakable bond they forged through the shared experience of parenthood. They learned to anticipate each other's needs, to offer support without being asked, to navigate the challenges of sleepless nights and overflowing diaper pails with a quiet efficiency that spoke volumes about the strength of their partnership.

Sira's anxieties, which had once been focused on Keith's ex-girlfriends and their lingering presence in his life, now centered on Maya's well-being. The constant worry gnawed at her, fueling a low-level anxiety that Keith recognized and patiently addressed. He learned to listen, truly listen, to her fears and insecurities, offering reassurance and practical support. He understood now that her earlier concerns, which he'd initially dismissed, stemmed from a deep-seated insecurity, an insecurity that had been amplified by the immense responsibility of motherhood. He saw the weight of the world on her shoulders, and he silently vowed to lighten the load.

One evening, as Keith soothed Maya back to sleep, Sira sat beside him, her hand resting gently on his arm. "I never thought it would be like this," she confessed, her voice hushed. "All the books, the magazines, the advice – none of it really prepared me."

Keith smiled, a soft, understanding smile that reached his eyes. "No," he agreed. "Nothing truly prepares you for this. But we're doing it, together. And we'll figure it out, together."

Their teamwork was evident in everything they did. They divided the tasks, not rigidly, but fluidly, adapting to the changing demands of their daughter's needs and their own individual capabilities. Keith excelled at the practical aspects of childcare – changing diapers, preparing bottles, soothing Maya's cries – while Sira found solace and fulfillment in the quieter moments, the gentle rocking, the whispered lullabies, the silent communion of mother and child. They complemented each other, their strengths balancing their weaknesses, creating a synergy that was both powerful and beautiful.

The financial pressures, which had once seemed insurmountable, eased somewhat. Keith's job provided a steady income, and they managed their expenses with a newfound frugality, prioritizing their needs over their wants. The house, initially a source of tension, became a haven, a sanctuary where they built a life, a family. The presence of Keith's ex-girlfriends faded into the background, their occasional interactions becoming less significant as their lives revolved around Maya. Their friendship continued, but it no longer overshadowed Keith and Sira's relationship. It was as though the arrival of their daughter had subtly shifted the balance, redefining priorities and realigning their focus.

As Maya grew, so did their love. It was a love forged in exhaustion, tested by sleepless nights and endless diaper changes, but strengthened by shared experiences, mutual support, and the unyielding bond they shared with their daughter. Their journey was far from over; they knew that parenthood presented an endless series of challenges, both big and small. But as they faced each challenge, hand in hand, they found a new depth in their love, a new appreciation for their commitment, and a renewed sense of purpose.

One evening, as they sat on the porch, watching the sunset paint the sky in hues of orange and pink, Keith gently brushed a stray strand of hair from Sira's face. "Remember when we thought buying this house was a big deal?" he asked, a smile playing on his lips.

Sira laughed, a soft, melodious sound. "Remember when I thought having a baby would be a walk in the park?"

They shared a look, a look that spoke volumes about the journey they had embarked on, the challenges they had overcome, and the love that had bound them together through it all. Their relationship had evolved, matured, transformed. It was no longer just about them; it was about them and Maya, their little family unit, bound together by the powerful, enduring force of love and parenthood.

The arrival of Maya had not only changed their lives; it had deepened and strengthened their bond. The initial anxieties and insecurities had been replaced by a quiet confidence, a shared understanding, a mutual respect that went beyond the romantic love they'd once shared. Their relationship, now firmly rooted in the shared responsibility of parenthood, was stronger, more resilient, more profound than they could have ever imagined.

They celebrated Maya's first smile, her first crawl, her first steps, each milestone a testament to their unwavering love and unwavering commitment to their little family. The challenges remained, but they were met with a newfound strength, a collaborative spirit, and an unwavering belief in their ability to overcome any obstacle together. Their lives were no longer just about two individuals navigating the complexities of adult life; they were about a family, a unit, building a life, building a future, building a legacy, together.

The future, they knew, held countless uncertainties. But as they gazed at their sleeping daughter, nestled safely in her crib, Keith and Sira felt a profound sense of peace, a quiet confidence in their ability to face whatever life threw their way. They had weathered the storms, navigated the choppy waters, and emerged stronger, more connected, and more deeply in love than ever before. They had found their family, and in that discovery, they found a love that was richer, deeper, and more meaningful than any love they had known before. It was a love that transcended romantic passion, extending into the realms of shared responsibility, unwavering commitment, and unconditional love, a love that grew stronger with each passing day, a love that would guide and sustain them through the ever-evolving journey of parenthood. The journey was far from over; their love story was still unfolding, chapter by chapter, but they were ready, together, to embrace whatever the future held. The challenges were daunting, the responsibilities immense, but with each other, and with their precious Maya, they knew they could face anything. Their love story, now infused with the sweetness of parenthood, was a testament to their resilience, their love, and the unbreakable bond that held their little family together. Their future, uncertain as it might be, was filled with the promise of a love story that would continue to unfold, chapter by chapter, a story of love, growth, and the enduring power of family.

Chapter 8:

Sleep Deprivation and Stress

The first few weeks after Maya's arrival were a blur of bleary-eyed exhaustion, punctuated by moments of overwhelming joy and utter disbelief. Sira had envisioned motherhood, romanticized it even, but the reality was far more brutal than any fairy tale. The sleep deprivation was a relentless assault, each night a battle against a tide of fatigue so profound it felt like she was wading through quicksand. Keith, bless his heart, tried his best, but even his valiant efforts couldn't fully compensate for the sheer physical and mental drain.

One day bled into the next, marked only by the rhythmic cries of their newborn, the whir of the breast pump, and the endless cycle of feeding, burping, changing, and soothing.

The house, once a symbol of their shared future, now felt like a battleground of discarded diapers, overflowing laundry baskets, and the lingering scent of formula. The meticulously crafted meal plans vanished, replaced by a chaotic scramble for whatever nourishment they could grab amidst the whirlwind of caring for their tiny daughter.

The stress wasn't just physical. It was a pervasive, gnawing anxiety that clung to Sira like a shadow. Every whimper, every cough, every slight change in Maya's temperature sent a jolt of panic through her. The fear of doing something wrong, of failing as a mother, was a constant companion. She found herself scrutinizing Maya's every move, fretting over her feeding schedule, and constantly questioning whether she was meeting her daughter's needs.

Keith, despite his best intentions, often missed the subtle cues of Sira's distress. He saw her exhaustion, of course, but he didn't always understand the depth of her anxiety.

His attempts to help were well-meaning but sometimes clumsy, adding to her frustration rather than alleviating it. Simple tasks, like making a cup of coffee or taking a quick shower, felt like insurmountable feats, pushing Sira further into a state of overwhelmed despair. The joy she felt in Maya's presence often warred with a deep-seated sense of inadequacy, a constant internal battle that left her feeling emotionally spent.

One particularly rough night, after a string of sleepless hours marked by Maya's incessant crying, Sira snapped. She was changing Maya's diaper when a wave of frustration, fueled by exhaustion and fear, crashed over her. She burst into tears, the sobs wracking her body. Keith, startled by her sudden outburst, rushed to her side, his own exhaustion evident in his worried eyes.

"What's wrong?" he asked gently, his voice thick with sleepiness.

"I can't do this, Keith," she choked out, her voice trembling. "I'm not good enough. I'm failing her."

Keith pulled her into a hug, his arms wrapping around her tightly. He held her close, letting her cry without interruption, absorbing the raw emotion that poured from her. For once, he didn't try to offer solutions or platitudes. He just held her, letting her know she wasn't alone in her struggle.

In the quiet aftermath of her breakdown, they finally talked. They talked about the unrelenting stress, the crushing weight of sleep deprivation, and the overwhelming fear that came with being responsible for another human life. They acknowledged their shortcomings, admitting they weren't always communicating effectively, that their individual anxieties were sometimes overshadowing their shared love and commitment.

It was a turning point. They realized that they couldn't navigate the challenges of parenthood alone. They needed help, they needed support, and they needed to be more patient and understanding with each other. They made a conscious decision to prioritize their relationship, knowing that their ability to support each other was crucial to their success as parents.

They started small. Keith took on more night feedings, allowing Sira to get a few extra hours of uninterrupted sleep. They created a more realistic schedule for themselves, embracing a less structured approach that allowed for flexibility and spontaneity. They made a conscious effort to communicate their feelings openly and honestly, avoiding the unspoken resentments that had previously been allowed to fester.

They also reached out for help. Sira's therapist became a lifeline, offering a safe space to process her anxieties and fears. Her sessions weren't just about coping with the stress of motherhood, but also about managing the complexities of their relationship, learning to effectively communicate their needs and expectations.

They enlisted the help of their families, who stepped up to provide much-needed respite and emotional support. Keith's mother offered to babysit once a week, allowing them both a much-needed break. Sira's parents visited, bringing meals and helping with household chores. This support network wasn't just about practical assistance; it was about building a community of support that helped them navigate the emotional rollercoaster of parenthood.

The postpartum period wasn't easy. There were still tough days, moments of despair, and occasional bouts of frustration. But the constant fear, the feeling of being utterly alone in their struggle, gradually subsided. They found solace in their shared love for Maya, in their growing understanding of each other, and in the support they found in their friends and family. They had weathered a storm, and although the future still held uncertainties, they faced them together, their bond strengthened by the crucible of parenthood. The exhaustion lingered, but now it was tempered by a deep sense of love, of accomplishment, and of shared resilience. The house might still be a little messy, the laundry might still be piling up, but in the midst of the chaos, there was a newfound appreciation for the beauty of the moment, for the miracle of life, and for the profound love that bound them together as parents.

The sleepless nights blurred together, each one a testament to their growing capacity for resilience. The anxieties, though still present, no longer held the same suffocating power. Sira learned to recognize her own triggers, to understand the subtle signs of her mounting stress. She practiced mindfulness techniques, focusing on her breath and on the present moment to help calm her racing thoughts. Keith, in turn, learned to be more attuned to her emotional needs, more sensitive to her unspoken anxieties. He listened more actively, offered a reassuring presence, and learned the subtle art of truly hearing her, not just listening to her words.

One evening, weeks later, as they sat together on the couch, Maya asleep in her bassinet, a quiet contentment settled between them. The exhaustion was still there, etched onto their faces, but their eyes held a new depth of understanding, a newfound appreciation for the unspoken bonds that held them together. They were tired, yes, but they were also stronger, more connected, and profoundly in love. The journey hadn't been easy, but they had navigated the rough patches, emerging on the other side with a deeper understanding of themselves, their relationship, and the profound love they shared for their daughter. The challenges of parenthood were far from over, but they faced the future, not with fear, but with a quiet confidence, knowing they had each other, and that together, they could navigate whatever lay ahead. The love story wasn't just about their romance; it was a testament to their resilience, their shared journey through the beautiful chaos of parenthood, and the enduring power of love amidst the trials and tribulations of life. Their bond, forged in the fires of sleepless nights and overwhelming anxieties, was now stronger than ever. They had found a new rhythm, a new normal, a new level of intimacy and understanding forged in the crucible of parenthood.

Relationship Strain

The quiet contentment of that evening was, unfortunately, short-lived. The exhaustion, which had initially bonded them, now became a wedge between them. The constant cycle of feeding, changing diapers, and soothing a crying baby eroded their individual identities, leaving them feeling more like exhausted automatons than the vibrant couple they once were. The spontaneity that had characterized their relationship before Maya's arrival was gone, replaced by a rigid schedule dictated by the needs of their infant daughter. Date nights were a distant memory, replaced by hurried meals eaten in front of the television, punctuated by the rhythmic cries of their baby monitor.

Sira, still recovering physically and emotionally from childbirth, felt a profound sense of loneliness. The overwhelming responsibility of caring for Maya felt like a heavy cloak, smothering her. Keith, despite his best intentions, struggled to understand the depth of her exhaustion and the emotional toll it was taking. He saw the physical demands, the sleepless nights, but he couldn't fully grasp the emotional landscape Sira was navigating – the hormonal fluctuations, the anxieties about her body, the fear of not being a good enough mother.

"I just feel like I've lost myself," Sira confessed one evening, her voice barely a whisper. They were sitting on the couch again, Maya fast asleep, but the peaceful atmosphere of weeks before was absent. The air crackled with unspoken tensions.

Keith, his face etched with fatigue, reached for her hand. "I know, honey. It's hard. But we're doing it together, right?" His words felt inadequate, even to him. He knew that 'doing it together' felt more like a shared burden than a shared joy.

His attempts at help often backfired. His well-intentioned efforts to relieve her burden sometimes came across as patronizing, or as a reminder of her inadequacies. He'd offer to change a diaper, but his clumsy handling of the situation would only increase Sira's frustration. He tried to take over nighttime feedings, but his inexperience left Sira feeling more anxious than relieved.

The weight of expectation pressed down on them. Sira felt the pressure to be the perfect mother, the image of effortless motherhood she'd seen portrayed in magazines and on social media. Keith, meanwhile, struggled to balance his work with his newfound paternal responsibilities. The house, once a symbol of their love and commitment, now felt like a battlefield, littered with scattered toys and overflowing laundry baskets.

Their communication, once so easy and fluid, became strained and stilted. Arguments erupted over the smallest things – the temperature of the baby's bath water, the best way to soothe Maya's colic, even the arrangement of toys in the living room. The simmering resentments, fueled by sleep deprivation and unrelenting stress, boiled over into bitter exchanges.

Sira felt increasingly isolated. Her friends, busy with their own lives, couldn't fully comprehend the all-consuming nature of motherhood. Even her therapist, while supportive, couldn't completely erase the overwhelming sense of being alone in her struggle. She longed for the carefree days before Maya, for the ease of communication and the shared laughter that had once defined their relationship.

Keith, too, felt the strain. He missed their spontaneous adventures, the late-night talks, the intimacy that had once defined their connection. He felt inadequate, a feeling amplified by Sira's growing distance. He tried to rekindle their romance, suggesting a night out, but Sira was too exhausted to even consider it. He bought her flowers, but they wilted before she even had time to put them in water.

Their sex life, once vibrant and passionate, became nonexistent. The exhaustion, the physical changes Sira had undergone, and the sheer lack of time and energy created a chasm between them. This lack of intimacy only further deepened the emotional distance that was growing between them. The physical intimacy that had once been a cornerstone of their relationship felt as distant as a memory from a past life.

One particularly tense evening, after a screaming match over a spilled bottle of formula, Sira broke down in tears. "I don't know if we can do this, Keith," she sobbed, her voice raw with exhaustion and despair. "I don't know if we can do this anymore."

Keith, seeing the raw pain etched on her face, felt a pang of guilt. He had been so focused on the practical aspects of parenthood that he had neglected the emotional needs of his partner, the woman he loved more than anything in the world.

"We will," he said, his voice soft and filled with remorse. "We will figure this out. We have to. For Maya, if for no one else." His words held a desperate plea, a promise to himself as much as to Sira. He knew that simply saying the words wasn't enough. He needed to take tangible steps to repair the damage that had been done, to rebuild their relationship from the foundations up.

He knew he had to start by listening, truly listening, to Sira's concerns and anxieties. He needed to acknowledge her feelings, to validate her experiences, and to understand that her struggles were real and valid. He needed to share the burden more equally, stepping up and taking on more of the childcare responsibilities, so Sira could have moments of rest and self-care. He understood that he needed to prioritize their relationship, to make time for each other, even if it meant sacrificing some sleep or making adjustments to their schedule.

The road ahead wouldn't be easy. Their relationship was bruised, tested, and weary. But amidst the exhaustion and the arguments, amidst the diapers and the sleepless nights, a flicker of hope remained. The love they shared, though battered and frayed, was still there, a tenacious ember refusing to be extinguished. The challenge now was to nurture that flame, to fan it into a blaze that would illuminate their way through the darkness, guiding them towards a future where they could once again find joy and connection, not just as parents, but as partners, lovers, and best friends.

He knew that rebuilding trust and intimacy wouldn't happen overnight. It would take time, patience, and a conscious effort from both of them. He looked at Sira, her face streaked with tears but her eyes still holding a spark of the love he cherished. He knew that this was a marathon, not a sprint, and that they would have to run it together, hand-in-hand, supporting each other every step of the way. The journey of parenthood had thrown them unexpected curveballs, but they were committed to navigating those hurdles together.

The next few weeks saw a gradual shift. Keith started taking on more responsibilities around the house and with Maya. He made a conscious effort to listen to Sira without interrupting, validating her feelings, and offering genuine support instead of trying to fix everything. He started small, taking over nighttime feedings for a few hours a week, giving Sira time to sleep or simply have some time to herself. He took Maya for walks in the park, giving Sira a rare moment of quiet solitude. He started leaving little notes of affection – a simple "I love you" scrawled on a napkin, a small gesture, but one that spoke volumes.

Slowly but surely, the distance between them began to shrink. The arguments became less frequent, replaced by quiet moments of shared affection and understanding. They started carving out small pockets of time for themselves, stolen moments snatched between diaper changes and feedings. A shared cup of coffee in the morning, a quiet conversation over a late-night bottle, a stolen kiss before falling asleep – these small acts of intimacy rekindled the embers of their love.

One evening, weeks later, as they sat on the couch, Maya peacefully asleep in her crib, Sira leaned her head against Keith's shoulder. A comfortable silence settled between them, filled only with the gentle rhythm of their breathing. The exhaustion was still present, but it no longer felt like a suffocating weight. Instead, it was a shared burden, a shared experience that had strengthened their bond rather than breaking it.

Their journey was far from over. The challenges of parenthood, and of maintaining a healthy relationship amidst those challenges, would continue to test them. But as they looked at each other, a newfound sense of hope filled their eyes. They had found their way back to each other, their love stronger and deeper than ever before, forged in the fires of sleepless nights and unwavering commitment. They had faced the storm, and emerged on the other side, their love intact, and their hearts more deeply connected. The love story wasn't just about their romance; it was a testament to their resilience, their shared journey through the beautiful chaos of parenthood, and the enduring power of love amidst the trials and tribulations of life. Their bond, forged in the fires of sleepless nights and overwhelming anxieties, was now stronger than ever. They had found a new rhythm, a new normal, a new level of intimacy and understanding forged in the crucible of parenthood.

Seeking Support

The exhaustion was a constant, a low hum of fatigue that vibrated through their days and nights. Keith, used to the spontaneity of his life before Maya, found himself struggling to adapt. He missed his late-night poker games with his friends, the impromptu trips to the bar, the simple freedom of his bachelor days. He loved Maya fiercely, but the relentless demands of parenthood felt like a suffocating weight, a constant pressure that threatened to crack the foundation of their relationship.

Sira, meanwhile, grappled with a different kind of exhaustion—the emotional kind. The hormonal shifts, the sleep deprivation, the overwhelming responsibility of caring for a newborn—it all coalesced into a relentless tide of anxiety that threatened to pull her under. The idealized version of motherhood she'd envisioned during her pregnancy—the blissful bonding moments, the effortless nurturing—had dissolved into a chaotic reality of screaming fits, endless feedings, and the constant fear of doing something wrong.

One particularly grueling morning, after a night punctuated by Maya's cries, Sira broke down. Keith, bleary-eyed and equally exhausted, watched helplessly as tears streamed down her face. He wanted to fix it, to make it all better, but he didn't know how. His attempts at comfort felt clumsy and inadequate, only adding to her frustration.

"I don't know what I'm doing, Keith," she whispered, her voice thick with tears. "I feel like I'm failing."

That was the turning point. The moment when Keith realized that he couldn't shoulder this burden alone. They needed help.

The first step was acknowledging their vulnerability. It wasn't easy. Keith, in particular, struggled with the idea of admitting weakness, of needing assistance. He'd always prided himself on his independence, his self-reliance. But looking at Sira, broken and overwhelmed, he knew he had to swallow his pride.

They started small. Keith's mother, a practical and loving woman, offered to come over once a week to help with chores and give Sira a much-needed break. It was a lifesaver. Having someone else handle the laundry, the dishes, the endless stream of baby bottles, allowed Sira to focus on bonding with Maya and regaining some semblance of normalcy.

Then, they reached out to their friends. Initially, Keith had been hesitant. He worried about imposing on their lives, about disrupting their routines. But his friends, to their credit, were incredibly supportive. They brought over meals, offered to watch Maya for a few hours, and simply listened when Keith and Sira needed to vent. The simple act of sharing their struggles, of knowing they weren't alone, was incredibly therapeutic.

The support wasn't limited to their social circle. Sira's therapist, whom she had initially consulted for pre-natal anxiety, proved to be a vital resource during this challenging period. She provided Sira with coping mechanisms for managing her anxiety, tools to navigate the emotional rollercoaster of motherhood, and a safe space to express her fears and frustrations without judgment. The therapist also helped them understand the impact of sleep deprivation on their emotional well-being and provided strategies for improving their sleep patterns. The therapist also helped them understand the challenges of adjusting to parenthood as a couple.

Beyond the practical help and emotional support, the most valuable aspect of reaching out was the sense of community it created. It reminded them that parenthood wasn't a solitary journey. They weren't isolated in their struggles. There was a network of support surrounding them, a web of friends and family ready to lend a hand, an ear, a shoulder to cry on.

But seeking help wasn't a one-time fix; it was an ongoing process. There were days when exhaustion still threatened to overwhelm them, when the weight of responsibility felt crushing. There were moments when their patience wore thin, when their arguments flared up, fueled by sleep deprivation and stress. But now, they had the tools to navigate these moments, strategies to cope with the challenges, and a support system to lean on when things got tough.

As weeks turned into months, a new rhythm emerged in their lives. They found ways to incorporate small moments of connection amidst the chaos of parenthood. A stolen kiss during a diaper change, a shared smile over Maya's gummy grin, a quiet conversation whispered after the baby had finally fallen asleep. These small moments, these fleeting glimpses of intimacy, were crucial in rekindling the spark that had seemed to flicker during the early days of parenthood.

The support they received wasn't just about practical help; it was about emotional reassurance. It validated their feelings, their struggles, and their anxieties. It reminded them that they weren't alone, that others had faced similar challenges and emerged stronger on the other side. It reinforced their belief in their capacity to navigate the complexities of parenthood and maintain a loving and supportive relationship amidst the chaos.

The journey wasn't easy. There were moments of doubt, moments of frustration, moments when the weight of responsibility threatened to crush them. But by reaching out, by seeking support from their loved ones and professionals, they discovered the power of community and the strength found in shared experiences. They learned to lean on each other, to rely on the love and support that surrounded them, and to recognize that seeking help wasn't a sign of weakness, but rather a testament to their resilience, their commitment, and their enduring love for each other and their daughter. They continued attending couple's therapy sessions, finding it a valuable space for open communication and resolving conflicts in a healthy manner. It provided a structured environment to address unresolved issues from the past and establish clear expectations for their future. The sessions also helped them understand each other's perspectives better, minimizing misunderstandings and fostering empathy.

The challenges didn't disappear overnight, but their approach changed. They learned to communicate their needs more effectively, to express their anxieties and frustrations without resorting to blame or resentment. They learned to prioritize their relationship, to carve out time for each other, even amidst the demands of parenthood. They discovered the importance of self-care, recognizing that they couldn't pour from an empty cup. They made a conscious effort to schedule regular date nights, even if it meant employing a babysitter or relying on family for support. These moments, however brief, were vital in nurturing their connection and reaffirming their commitment to each other.

The transformation wasn't immediate, but it was palpable. The constant tension that had initially defined their relationship began to ease. The exhaustion remained, but it was tempered by a newfound sense of teamwork, a shared understanding of their challenges, and a deep appreciation for the support system that surrounded them. They began to rediscover the joy in their relationship, the intimacy they'd once shared, and the deep love that bound them together. The challenges remained, of course, but now, they faced them hand-in-hand, their bond strengthened by the shared experience of parenthood and the unwavering support of their loved ones. They knew that the journey was far from over, but they faced the future with a renewed sense of hope, confidence, and a deeper, more resilient love than they had ever imagined possible.

The impact of this support extended beyond just Keith and Sira. Maya thrived in an environment of love and stability, surrounded by a network of caring individuals. The challenges of parenthood were still present, but their ability to manage them effectively transformed their family unit into a cohesive and supportive system. The experience taught them valuable lessons about the importance of communication, vulnerability, and seeking external aid when needed. It fostered a sense of reliance and collaboration that would continue to strengthen their relationship in the years to come. The struggles they had overcome served as a foundation for their future, a testament to their resilience, and a reminder that even in the face of adversity, love, support, and a willingness to seek help can overcome any obstacle. Their journey served as a powerful example of how seeking help is not a sign of weakness but a sign of strength and a commitment to building a healthy and happy family. The path to parenthood wasn't always easy, but with the help they sought and the love they shared, they were successfully navigating the beautiful chaos of raising their daughter and strengthening their bond as a couple. Their story was not just about overcoming challenges; it was about the transformation of their love, strengthened by shared experiences and unwavering support.

Redefining Roles

The first few months after Maya's arrival were a blur of sleepless nights, overflowing diapers, and a constant battle against the relentless tide of exhaustion. Sira, despite the initial joy, found herself grappling with a profound sense of loss. The Sira she knew, the independent, carefree college student, felt like a distant memory. Her identity, once so firmly rooted in her own ambitions and aspirations, now seemed inextricably intertwined with her role as a mother. This shift, while entirely natural, felt overwhelming at times. She missed the spontaneity of her life before Maya, the freedom to pursue her passions without the constant demands of a tiny human.

Keith, too, was undergoing a transformation. The easygoing charm that had once captivated Sira was now tempered by a deeper sense of responsibility. He found himself fiercely protective of his daughter, his every action dictated by a love so profound it both exhilarated and terrified him. He loved Sira deeply, but the relentless pressure of parenthood strained their relationship in unexpected ways. His attempts to maintain his pre-fatherhood lifestyle clashed with Sira's exhaustion and fluctuating emotions. Their arguments, once playful disagreements, now held a sharper edge, fueled by sleep deprivation and the immense pressure they both felt.

One particularly fraught evening, after a particularly grueling day punctuated by Maya's incessant crying, Sira confessed her fears to Keith. "I feel like I've lost myself," she whispered, tears tracing paths down her cheeks. "I'm just…a mom. That's all I am now."

Keith, his own exhaustion evident in the dark circles under his eyes, reached out to take her hand. "That's not true, Sira," he said softly. "You're still Sira. You're an amazing mom, but you're so much more than that. You're intelligent, funny, strong…you're everything I love about you, and Maya loves you too."

His words, though heartfelt, weren't enough to fully quell her anxieties. Sira needed more than reassurance; she needed to rediscover herself, to find a balance between her role as a mother and her own individual identity. She began incorporating small acts of self-care into her daily routine, carving out pockets of time for herself amidst the chaos of parenthood. She started reading again, indulging in books that transported her away from the relentless demands of motherhood. She reconnected with old friends, finding solace in their company and a renewed sense of normalcy.

For Keith, the adjustment was equally challenging. He had always valued his independence, his friendships, his freedom. Now, those things felt distant, almost unattainable. He missed his late-night poker games, the carefree camaraderie of his friends, the simple pleasure of a spontaneous night out. He felt a growing resentment towards the constraints of parenthood, a resentment he struggled to reconcile with his immense love for his daughter.

Their shared struggle brought them closer in some ways and further apart in others. They learned to communicate their needs more openly, to acknowledge their frustrations and anxieties without judgment. They found ways to share the burden of childcare, to create a system that allowed them both moments of respite and personal time. Keith started taking on more household chores, even learning how to change diapers with a surprising level of competence. Sira, in turn, made an effort to involve Keith more actively in Maya's care, realizing that his involvement was crucial not only for her well-being but for their relationship.

The changes weren't immediate or effortless. There were still arguments, moments of frustration, and feelings of inadequacy. But they were learning, adapting, growing together. They were redefining their roles not just as parents but as a couple, navigating the uncharted territory of parenthood with a newfound appreciation for each other's strengths and vulnerabilities. They discovered that their love, initially a whirlwind of passion and excitement, was now forged in the crucible of shared challenges, strengthened by their unwavering commitment to each other and their daughter.

One evening, while Maya slept soundly in her crib, Keith and Sira sat on the couch, sipping tea and watching a quiet movie. The exhaustion was still there, a persistent undercurrent to their lives, but it felt different now. It wasn't a weight threatening to crush them; it was a shared experience that bound them together. They had found a rhythm, a balance, a new definition of their roles.

Sira, looking at Keith, saw not just the man she had fallen in love with, but a partner who was evolving alongside her, a father who loved their daughter fiercely, and a man who was learning to navigate the complexities of parenthood with grace and determination. She felt a profound sense of gratitude, not just for the man beside her, but for the journey they had undertaken together.

Keith, in turn, looked at Sira, seeing not just the woman who had given him a child, but a partner who was stronger and more resilient than he had ever imagined. He saw a woman who had redefined her own identity, who had found a way to balance motherhood with her own aspirations and dreams. He saw a woman he loved even more deeply than before.

Their journey was far from over. Parenthood, they knew, was a lifelong journey, filled with both joys and challenges. But they were ready to face those challenges together, hand in hand, their bond strengthened by the crucible of shared experiences and their unwavering commitment to each other and their precious daughter, Maya.

The arrival of Maya had irrevocably changed their lives, their individual identities, and the dynamic of their relationship. But it also brought a depth of love and connection they hadn't known was possible. It was a love born of shared sacrifice, unwavering support, and a willingness to navigate the uncharted waters of parenthood together. They had redefined their roles, not just as parents, but as partners, learning to support each other's dreams while nurturing the life they had created together. The future held uncertainties, but they faced them with a newfound confidence, their hearts filled with the unwavering love that bound them together as a family.

The redefinition of their roles extended beyond their immediate family unit. Sira's relationship with her own parents evolved, transforming from a daughter-parent dynamic to one of collaborative support. Her parents, initially apprehensive about Sira's young motherhood, stepped in to provide crucial childcare assistance, offering respite and a renewed sense of normalcy for both Sira and Keith. This intergenerational support system proved invaluable, creating a stronger family network.

Similarly, Keith's relationship with his friends shifted. Initially, he felt a sense of distance and alienation from his old life, but as time went on, his friends began to understand and accept the changes in his life. They became involved in Maya's life, offering support and creating a sense of community around the new family. This understanding and acceptance helped to bridge the gap between Keith's old life and his new reality as a father, reinforcing the importance of healthy social connections even amidst the demands of parenthood.

The challenges continued, of course. Financial pressures remained, forcing Keith and Sira to make sacrifices and reassess their priorities. They learned to budget more effectively, to prioritize their needs, and to find creative solutions to overcome financial hurdles. This shared struggle further strengthened their bond, demonstrating their ability to work together towards common goals.

Moreover, the emotional toll of parenthood was ongoing. There were days filled with overwhelming exhaustion, moments of self-doubt, and the constant pressure to be perfect parents. They learned to acknowledge these feelings, to validate their emotional experiences, and to seek support when needed. They attended parenting classes, joined support groups, and continued their therapy sessions, finding solace and practical advice in these shared experiences.

The unexpected visit from Sira's high school ex-boyfriend, while initially jarring, ultimately served as a catalyst for further growth and understanding. It forced Keith and Sira to confront their pasts and to reaffirm their commitment to their present relationship. It was a reminder that navigating adulthood and parenthood was a continual process, requiring constant communication, trust, and a willingness to confront their own insecurities and vulnerabilities.

Ultimately, Keith and Sira's journey through parenthood was not just about overcoming challenges, but about the evolution of their love and the strengthening of their bond. It was a testament to the power of shared experiences, unwavering support, and the willingness to constantly adapt and redefine their roles within their evolving family unit. The path wasn't always easy, but the love they shared, nurtured through the shared struggles and triumphs of parenthood, made their journey not only survivable, but beautifully fulfilling. Their story became a beacon of hope, a testament to the resilience of love and the transformative power of family. It showed that while the path of parenthood is often challenging and unpredictable, it is also one of immense growth, love and profound connection, leaving readers with a sense of inspiration and encouragement.

The Balancing Act

The first tentative steps toward regaining a sense of balance felt like navigating a minefield blindfolded. Sira, still reeling from the initial shock of motherhood, realized that her identity wasn't simply erased; it was just… rearranged. She was still Sira, but now she was also Maya's mother. That wasn't a loss, she finally understood, but a profound expansion. The key was to find a way to integrate these different facets of herself without feeling overwhelmed.

Keith, initially oblivious to the subtle shifts in Sira's emotional landscape, began to notice. He saw the exhaustion etched on her face, the way her eyes held a flicker of something lost. It wasn't the radiant joy of new parenthood he'd expected; it was something deeper, more complex. He'd assumed the challenges would be solely logistical – the sleepless nights, the constant feeding, the endless laundry – but he hadn't anticipated the profound emotional toll on Sira. He started paying attention, truly listening, not just to her words, but to the unspoken anxieties that clouded her eyes.

Their first attempt at finding equilibrium was disastrous. Keith, driven by a desire to "help," insisted on taking over nighttime feedings. He envisioned himself as the knight in shining armor, rescuing Sira from the relentless cycle of sleep deprivation. The reality, however, was less romantic. His clumsy attempts at burping Maya resulted in a symphony of gurgles and frustrated sighs, culminating in a projectile vomit incident that landed squarely on his favorite shirt. Sira, despite her initial gratitude, found herself constantly correcting his techniques, leading to a simmering tension that quickly escalated into a full-blown argument. The attempt to "share the load" only served to add more stress to an already precarious situation.

Their therapist, Dr. Anya Sharma, had offered invaluable insight. She helped them understand that balance wasn't about perfectly dividing responsibilities, but about creating a flexible system that acknowledged their individual needs and strengths. She emphasized the importance of open communication and mutual respect, urging them to identify their individual breaking points and create strategies to avoid them. Sira, for example, needed uninterrupted time for herself, even if it was just a few minutes to read a book or take a long bath. Keith, on the other hand, thrived on physical activity and found solace in long runs.

Implementing Dr. Sharma's advice was a slow, iterative process. They started small, scheduling dedicated "me time" for each other, even if it meant sacrificing sleep or delegating chores. Sira discovered that even fifteen minutes of quiet contemplation could rejuvenate her spirit, allowing her to approach motherhood with renewed energy. Keith, understanding the importance of Sira's emotional well-being, took on more household chores, ensuring that she had the time and space she needed. This wasn't a flawless system; there were days when exhaustion won, when arguments erupted, and when the delicate balance tilted precariously. But each time they stumbled, they learned to pick themselves up, to communicate their needs more effectively, and to adjust their approach accordingly.

The financial strain, a constant undercurrent in their lives, continued to pose a challenge. Keith's job, while stable, didn't provide the financial cushion they'd hoped for. The cost of childcare, coupled with the ever-increasing expenses associated with raising a child, was daunting. Sira, despite her initial reluctance, finally agreed to return to freelance work, albeit on a limited scale. She found a niche writing children's stories, a project that allowed her to balance her creative aspirations with her maternal responsibilities. It wasn't the glamorous career she'd envisioned in college, but it was a compromise that brought her a sense of accomplishment and financial independence.

The presence of Keith's ex-girlfriends, a source of constant tension for Sira, also became a point of discussion. They had reached a point where they had accepted the reality of these existing friendships; but understanding did not equate to approval. The key, they discovered, was communication, and setting boundaries. Keith was careful to always be transparent about who he was with and what he was doing; and he made sure to always include Sira in his social gatherings when appropriate. They were working on building a secure home and a loving relationship within that framework, and Sira had decided to allow Keith's pre-existing relationships to co-exist – as long as those relationships didn't infringe on the sanctity and safety of their newly established family unit.

The re-emergence of Sira's high school ex-boyfriend, Mark, added an unexpected layer of complexity. Mark's visit, initially framed as a casual catch-up, stirred up dormant feelings and insecurities. Sira, caught off guard by the intensity of her reaction, confided in Keith. Their initial reaction to this new challenge was one of mistrust; but after a long conversation, they realized this was an opportunity for them to confront their fears, to deepen their understanding of each other, and to solidify their commitment. This was not to diminish the shock of having someone from their past resurface; but in the grand scheme of things, it served as a catalyst for them to confront the deepest issues that were still lingering.

Their journey toward a balanced life was a testament to their resilience, their unwavering commitment, and their ability to adapt to life's unexpected twists and turns. They learned to embrace the messy realities of parenthood, to celebrate their individual strengths, and to nurture their love amidst the chaos. It wasn't a perfect equilibrium, but it was theirs – a dynamic, ever-evolving balance forged in the crucible of shared experiences, mutual support, and a deep, abiding love. They acknowledged the inevitable imperfections, and embraced the beauty found in the journey itself. This was their journey; and their new normal.

Their daily routine gradually evolved into a choreography of shared responsibilities and individual pursuits. Keith, after learning to change diapers and soothe Maya with the expertise of a seasoned pro, took on the mornings. He'd get Maya ready, ensuring she was fed, changed, and happy before leaving for work. Sira, fueled by her newfound creative energy, dedicated her mornings to her writing, finding solace in the rhythmic tap-tap-tap of her keyboard, the words flowing onto the page. Evenings were dedicated to family time, a sacred space where they'd read stories to Maya, play games, and simply enjoy each other's company.

They discovered the power of small gestures, the unspoken language of love conveyed through a shared glance, a gentle touch, a cup of coffee made just the way the other person liked it. These were the tiny threads that wove together the fabric of their lives, strengthening their bond with each passing day. The challenges remained, of course; there were still moments of frustration, arguments, and exhaustion. But they approached these setbacks with a newfound wisdom, a shared understanding that their journey was about progress, not perfection. They knew that stumbling was part of the dance, that falling and getting back up, together, was the very essence of their evolving relationship.

Sira and Keith's story wasn't just about navigating the challenges of parenthood; it was about the evolution of their love, the deepening of their connection, and the unwavering support they provided each other. It was a journey of self-discovery, resilience and adaptation. They learned to value the importance of open communication, mutual respect, and a willingness to compromise. They discovered that balance wasn't about an equal division of responsibilities, but about creating a flexible system that accommodated their individual needs and strengths, acknowledging that the concept of "balance" was itself a dynamic and constantly evolving state.

They learned to prioritize their relationship, scheduling date nights, even if it meant hiring a babysitter for a few hours. These moments, away from the demands of parenthood, allowed them to reconnect, to reaffirm their commitment, and to remember the love that had brought them together in the first place. They realized that a strong relationship wasn't something that was simply maintained; it was something that needed constant nurturing, attention, and a willingness to adapt as their lives changed and evolved. Their success lay not in eliminating the challenges, but in learning to face them together, to support each other, and to find joy in the shared journey. Their relationship, once fragile and tested, had grown stronger, deeper, and more resilient than they had ever imagined. The path had been fraught with difficulties, but it was a testament to the transformative power of love, perseverance, and the shared commitment to building a life together. And through it all, Maya, their precious daughter, remained the center of their universe, the guiding star that illuminated their path toward a future filled with love, laughter, and a uniquely theirs, imperfectly perfect balance.

Chapter 9:

Overcoming Obstacles

The first few months after the baby's arrival were a blur of sleepless nights, overflowing diaper pails, and a constant, low-level hum of anxiety. Sira, despite the overwhelming joy of motherhood, found herself grappling with a postpartum depression she hadn't anticipated. The idyllic picture of parenthood she'd painted in her mind was crumbling under the weight of reality. The constant demands of a newborn felt like a relentless assault, leaving her feeling depleted and emotionally fragile. Keith, bless his heart, tried his best. He helped with diaper changes, bottle feedings (when the baby would cooperate), and even managed to conquer the terrifying beast that was the baby swing assembly. But even his unwavering support couldn't fully alleviate the pressure Sira felt. She felt guilty for feeling overwhelmed, for the moments when the baby's cries grated on her nerves, for the exhaustion that threatened to consume her entirely.

One particularly brutal night, after a three-hour feeding marathon punctuated by screaming and spit-up, Sira broke down. She confessed to Keith, tears streaming down her face, that she felt like a failure. She wasn't the serene, confident mother she'd imagined she would be. She felt inadequate, clumsy, and utterly lost in the sea of parental responsibilities. Keith, for the first time, really saw her. He saw past the exhaustion, the frazzled hair, and the stained pajamas to the vulnerable woman underneath. He gently held her, whispering words of reassurance and understanding. He admitted his own struggles, acknowledging the pressure he'd been feeling to provide financially and emotionally for their growing family. That night, they didn't just talk about the baby; they talked about themselves, their fears, and their hopes for the future. It was a turning point.

Their communication became more honest and open. They started attending couples' therapy, a decision they'd initially hesitated on but ultimately proved invaluable. The therapist helped them identify unhealthy communication patterns and develop healthier ways of expressing their needs and concerns. They learned to actively listen, to validate each other's feelings, and to approach disagreements with empathy instead of defensiveness. Sira continued her individual therapy, working through her postpartum depression and exploring her evolving identity as a mother. She started a support group for new mothers, connecting with other women who shared similar experiences and offered invaluable solidarity and practical advice.

The financial strain remained a significant challenge. The house Keith had bought felt less like a dream home and more like a constant reminder of their financial burden. They tightened their belts, cut expenses wherever possible, and Keith picked up extra shifts at his job. Sira, once she felt a little stronger emotionally and physically, started freelancing as a graphic designer, utilizing her skills to earn some extra income. It wasn't easy, but working together, they found a way to navigate the financial difficulties and create a more stable foundation for their family.

The reappearance of Sira's high school ex-boyfriend, Mark, had initially caused a significant rift between Sira and Keith. Mark's reappearance stirred up old feelings and insecurities. However, instead of letting jealousy consume him, Keith took a different approach. He sat down with Sira and listened, really listened, to her feelings about Mark. He understood that Mark represented a piece of Sira's past, not a threat to their present. He worked on processing his own jealousy, acknowledging its roots in his own insecurities about his worthiness of Sira's love. Their relationship benefited from the renewed understanding about communication and mutual respect.

The presence of Keith's ex-girlfriends continued to be a source of tension for Sira, but over time, she learned to see them not as rivals but as a part of Keith's past, a past that didn't diminish their present relationship. She began to understand that Keith's friendships with his exes weren't a reflection of his feelings for her, but rather a testament to his capacity for maintaining healthy, respectful relationships. She acknowledged that her own insecurities stemmed from her own past experiences and learned to communicate those insecurities honestly with Keith. He, in turn, made an effort to alleviate her anxieties, assuring her of his love and commitment. He even started inviting her to casual gatherings with his friends, including his exes, demonstrating his willingness to include her in his life fully. These interactions were initially uncomfortable for

Sira but eventually helped her to feel more secure and included in Keith's world.

Their relationship wasn't magically fixed overnight. There were still disagreements, moments of frustration, and the occasional sleepless night filled with whispered anxieties. But the foundation of their relationship had become stronger, forged in the fires of their challenges. They learned to communicate more effectively, to truly listen to each other's concerns, and to approach conflicts with empathy and understanding. They learned the importance of actively seeking support from each other, from family, and from professionals.

As their child grew, their roles and responsibilities evolved. Keith, always the provider, discovered a deep and unexpected wellspring of patience and tenderness in his role as a father. Sira, initially overwhelmed by the demands of motherhood, discovered her own strength, resilience, and a love that surpassed anything she could have ever imagined. They learned to adapt to changing circumstances, to adjust their expectations, and to appreciate the smaller moments of joy amidst the chaos.

Overcoming the obstacles wasn't about magically erasing the challenges but about learning to navigate them together, with honesty, compassion, and a deep commitment to their love. They celebrated milestones – the first smile, the first steps, the first words – not just as parents but as partners, their bond strengthened by the shared experience of raising their child. They learned that true love wasn't about a fairytale romance; it was about facing life's complexities together, hand in hand, supporting each other through every triumph and tribulation. They discovered that resilience wasn't about the absence of hardship, but about the strength to rise above it, together. And in that shared struggle, their love deepened, becoming more profound, more resilient, and more meaningful than ever before. The future held new challenges, undoubtedly, but they faced them not with fear, but with a quiet confidence born from the battles they had already won, together. Their journey was far from over, but they were ready, prepared, and deeply in love, ready to face whatever came next, hand in hand, as a family. The journey had been arduous, but the destination—a strengthened bond, a loving family, and a deep-seated commitment to overcoming any obstacle—was worth every struggle. Their love story was not just a romance, but a testament to the enduring power of commitment, resilience, and the transformative force of love in the face of adversity. The path had been challenging, but it had brought them to a stronger, more resilient, and deeply loving place. The future was bright, filled with the promise of a life lived together, not just as lovers, but as parents, as friends, as a family unit bound by a love forged in the crucible of life's trials and tribulations.

Strengthening Bonds

The arrival of their daughter, Maya, marked a turning point. The initial chaos of sleepless nights and hormonal imbalances gradually subsided, replaced by a quieter, more profound understanding between Sira and Keith. The constant pressure of parenthood, initially a source of friction, became a crucible in which their love was refined and strengthened. Sira, finally able to articulate the depth of her postpartum anxieties to Keith, found him more receptive than she'd ever imagined. He listened, not with the patronizing sympathy she'd sometimes felt from well-meaning friends, but with genuine empathy and a willingness to learn.

He began to understand the subtle shifts in her mood, the exhaustion that went beyond physical fatigue, the overwhelming sense of responsibility that threatened to suffocate her. He took on more household chores, not because she asked, but because he saw the strain on her face, the exhaustion in her eyes. He learned to anticipate her needs, to bring her a cup of tea before she even realized she was thirsty, to take the baby for an extra hour so she could steal a nap. These small acts of service weren't grand gestures, but they spoke volumes about the depth of his love and his unwavering commitment to supporting her.

Their therapy sessions continued, but now they were less about resolving individual anxieties and more about navigating the challenges of parenthood as a team. The therapist helped them develop healthy communication strategies, tools to manage conflict constructively, and strategies for sharing the emotional burden of raising a child. They learned to identify their individual stress triggers and to find ways to mitigate them, understanding that their individual well-being was intrinsically linked to the strength of their relationship.

Sira, having worked through her anxieties, found herself appreciating Keith's strengths in a new light. His initially clumsy attempts to understand her postpartum depression had evolved into a genuine effort to support her emotionally and practically. His commitment to providing for their family wasn't just about finances; it was a testament to his dedication to their shared future, to their little family unit. He even surprised her by enrolling in a parenting class, a move that both amused and touched her. He was making a conscious effort to be the best partner and father he could be, and that meant continuous learning and adaptation.

Meanwhile, the issue of Keith's ex-girlfriends, once a significant source of tension, seemed to fade into the background. Sira realized that her insecurities stemmed not from their friendships, but from her own anxieties about her self-worth. With the support of Keith and her therapist, she learned to trust herself and her relationship. She came to understand that Keith's relationships with his exes were firmly in the past, that his love for her was genuine and unwavering. The women, seeing Sira's strength and resilience, became less of a threat and more like a supportive part of Keith's broader social circle. They offered friendly advice and shared experiences, making the transition into motherhood less isolating for Sira.

The surprise visit from Sira's high school ex-boyfriend, initially a cause for concern, ultimately proved to be a non-issue. The young man, now a different person altogether, had simply wanted to catch up and express his admiration for how far Sira had come. The encounter highlighted the growth Sira had experienced since high school; she was confident, secure, and completely committed to her life with Keith and Maya. The memory of their past felt distant, almost irrelevant. It underscored the transformation that she had undertaken, a journey that Keith had been a constant support in.

Their family life wasn't without its bumps and scrapes. There were still sleepless nights, tantrums, and the inevitable disagreements that come with co-parenting. But these challenges no longer felt insurmountable. They learned to face them with a new sense of unity and cooperation, a testament to the deep bond that had grown between them. Their relationship wasn't simply a romantic partnership; it had evolved into a profound connection, a resilient family unit that thrived in the face of adversity.

Their connection deepened through shared responsibilities. Keith learned the soothing rhythms of rocking Maya to sleep, the art of changing a diaper with minimal fuss, and the patience required to soothe a crying infant. Sira, in turn, found herself appreciating Keith's unwavering support, his willingness to take on the less glamorous aspects of parenthood, and his unwavering love for her and their daughter.

They found moments of joy amidst the chaos. The first tentative smile, Maya's first steps, her first attempts at babbling – these were milestones celebrated not just as individual achievements but as a testament to their collective effort, to the strength of their bond as parents. They learned to appreciate the small things – a shared cup of coffee in the early morning, a stolen moment of intimacy in the midst of the day's whirlwind.

Evenings became their time. After Maya was asleep, they would sit together, often in comfortable silence, sometimes engaging in light-hearted conversation. These moments were precious, a quiet refuge from the demands of parenthood. They reflected on their journey, on the obstacles they had overcome, and on the love that had bound them together. They talked about dreams for the future, dreams that now included Maya, dreams that were bigger and more ambitious because of the foundation they had built together.

Keith, having initially struggled with the complexities of Sira's emotional journey, began to understand the depth of his own feelings. He realized that his love for Sira was not just a romantic ideal, but a deep-seated commitment to her well-being, to her happiness, to their shared future. His support for Sira wasn't just an act of generosity, it was a reflection of his own personal growth, his evolution as a partner and as a man. He embraced his role as a father not with a sense of obligation, but with a profound sense of love and responsibility.

Their bond strengthened further through acts of forgiveness and understanding. Sira, having forgiven Keith for his initial lack of understanding regarding her postpartum depression, felt a deep sense of peace and contentment. Keith, in turn, forgave Sira for her initial anxieties and insecurities, realizing that her concerns stemmed from a place of love and a deep desire for their family's well-being. This mutual forgiveness was the foundation of a stronger, more resilient relationship.

Their journey was far from over. The path ahead would certainly be filled with new challenges, new anxieties, and unforeseen obstacles. But they faced the future with a quiet confidence, a deep-seated trust in their love, and an unwavering commitment to their family. Their relationship was no longer just a romance; it was a partnership, a testament to the power of resilience, a foundation built on mutual respect, understanding, and an enduring love that had weathered the storm and emerged stronger than ever. Their story was a testament to the fact that love, like life itself, is a journey, not a destination. And this journey, although challenging, was theirs, shared hand-in-hand, step-by-step, every moment a celebration of their enduring love, a love that had transformed into something even deeper and more meaningful with the arrival of their child, Maya. Their love story, a contemporary romance amidst the chaos of parenthood, was far from its end; instead, it had just begun its next chapter, full of promise and hope.

Emotional Maturity

The first few months after Maya's arrival were a blur of exhaustion, punctuated by moments of pure, overwhelming joy. Sira, initially hesitant to admit it, even to herself, found a surprising strength within her. The anxieties that had plagued her during pregnancy – anxieties Keith had initially dismissed as irrational – slowly began to dissipate. This wasn't a magical transformation; it was a gradual process, fueled by the unwavering support Keith offered. He wasn't perfect, of course. He still had his moments of clumsiness, his attempts at helpfulness sometimes veering into unhelpful territory. But his willingness to learn, to listen, to truly see Sira's struggles, was a revelation. He started taking initiative, researching postpartum depression, understanding her hormonal fluctuations, even learning how to soothe Maya's cries more effectively than Sira herself. This active participation in her emotional journey was the keystone to their growth.

One evening, while Maya slept soundly in her bassinet, Sira confessed her lingering insecurities about their relationship. The shadow of Keith's ex-girlfriends still loomed, a faint but persistent unease in the back of her mind. This time, Keith didn't offer platitudes or dismiss her feelings. He listened, patiently, his gaze soft and understanding. He admitted that he hadn't fully grasped the depth of her pain before, blinded by his own insecurities and the belief that he was doing everything right. He explained that his friendships with his exes were platonic, born of shared history and mutual respect, nothing more. He assured her that his love for her, for them, was absolute, a steadfast beacon in the sometimes turbulent waters of their lives. This conversation, raw and honest, laid bare their vulnerabilities, forging a stronger bond between them. It was a turning point not only in their romantic relationship but in their communication as well. They learned to articulate their needs and concerns without fear of judgment, creating a safe space for open and honest dialogue.

Sira's therapy sessions continued, proving invaluable in her journey of self-discovery. She explored the root of her insecurities, uncovering deeply ingrained patterns of self-doubt stemming from her childhood. With the therapist's guidance, she learned to challenge these negative thought patterns, replacing them with affirmations of self-worth and resilience. This newfound self-awareness permeated all aspects of her life, empowering her in her role as a mother and strengthening her relationship with Keith. She understood that her anxieties weren't a personal failing, but a natural response to the immense changes in her life. She began to embrace her vulnerability, recognizing it not as weakness, but as a testament to her capacity for love and connection.

Keith, too, underwent a significant personal transformation. He realized that his initial dismissal of Sira's anxieties stemmed from his own fear of inadequacy. He had always prided himself on his independence, his ability to handle everything on his own. The arrival of Maya, and the subsequent challenges of parenthood, forced him to confront his limitations, to acknowledge his dependence on Sira and, more importantly, to embrace it. He learned to appreciate her strength, her resilience, and the unwavering love that she poured into their family. His friendships with his exes continued, but with a new perspective. He understood that these relationships, previously a source of tension, could coexist with his love for Sira, without compromising his loyalty or commitment. He found a mature way to navigate these complex relationships, prioritizing their family and fostering mutual respect with those in his past.

Their financial situation, a persistent source of stress, also began to improve. Keith's career was taking off, and the initial strain of house ownership eased. They meticulously budgeted, making conscious choices about their spending, finding joy in small pleasures and appreciating the abundance they had, both materially and emotionally. They celebrated small victories – a successful family dinner, a peaceful evening spent reading together, a spontaneous moment of laughter with Maya. They began to value quality time over material possessions, understanding that the richness of their lives wasn't measured in dollars but in shared moments of love and connection.

The surprise visit from Sira's high school ex-boyfriend, Mark, initially stirred up a storm of mixed emotions. Sira, initially hesitant, found herself surprisingly composed. She saw Mark as a relic of her past, a reminder of a time when she was less confident, less secure. She appreciated the opportunity to acknowledge that past, but firmly affirmed her present reality. The conversation was short and amicable, void of any romantic undertones. Keith, initially apprehensive, watched the interaction unfold with surprise and newfound confidence in Sira and in their relationship. He understood that Sira's past relationships didn't diminish her present love for him. It was a testament to her journey, to her growth and maturity.

Their emotional maturity extended beyond their relationship; it manifested in their roles as parents. They made conscious decisions about their parenting style, prioritizing open communication, mutual respect, and a loving, supportive environment for Maya. They recognized their own imperfections, acknowledging that they would make mistakes along the way. This self-awareness enabled them to learn from their errors, adapt their parenting strategies, and cultivate a deeper understanding of their daughter's needs. They learned to communicate their frustrations and anxieties without resorting to blame or criticism, fostering a healthy and positive family dynamic. They created rituals and routines that brought them closer – bedtime stories, family dinners, weekend adventures. These seemingly small gestures built a strong foundation for their family, solidifying their roles as parents and partners.

The transition to parenthood wasn't just about diapers and sleepless nights; it was about navigating a complex emotional landscape, about facing their own insecurities and vulnerabilities, and about emerging stronger and more resilient than before. It was a journey of self-discovery, a process of growth and healing, culminating in a profound and unshakeable love that transcended the initial romantic spark. Their love story wasn't a fairytale; it was a realistic portrayal of a relationship tested by the trials and tribulations of adult life, shaped by the triumphs and struggles of parenthood, and ultimately strengthened by their shared commitment to love, understanding, and unwavering support for each other. The journey had its bumps and detours, but it was a journey they were taking hand-in-hand, their love serving as the compass guiding them toward a future filled with promise and hope. The arrival of Maya had not only expanded their family; it had transformed them as individuals, making them stronger, more compassionate, and more deeply in love than ever before. Their love story was a testament to the enduring power of resilience, a powerful narrative of growth, healing, and the enduring magic of finding your person amidst the chaos of life. Their future, while uncertain, was a bright canvas upon which they would paint their love story, one brushstroke of shared moments, laughter, and unwavering devotion at a time. Their story was a love letter to the journey, a testament to the fact that love, like life itself, is a constant evolution, a dance between challenges and triumphs, a story always unfolding, forever in progress.

Shared Dreams and Goals

The first tentative steps toward creating a shared future began subtly, woven into the fabric of their daily routines. It started with small things – a whispered conversation late at night, nestled between feedings and diaper changes, about what kind of garden they'd plant in their backyard once Maya was a little older. Sira, ever practical, envisioned rows of tomatoes and herbs, enough to fill their pantry with homemade goodness. Keith, with his boundless energy, dreamed of a sprawling vegetable patch, complete with a tiny scarecrow Maya could decorate. These seemingly insignificant exchanges held a profound weight, a silent acknowledgment that they were building something together, something that extended beyond their immediate circumstances.

One evening, as Maya slept soundly in her bassinet, Keith traced the lines of Sira's tired but contented face.

"Remember that old sketchbook of mine?" he asked, a mischievous glint in his eyes. Sira chuckled, remembering the countless doodles and half-formed ideas that filled its pages. "The one filled with half-finished spaceship designs and bizarre creatures?"

He nodded. "I've been thinking... maybe we could start working on it together. Maybe Maya will inherit my artistic gene." He winked, adding a touch of humor to a sentiment that spoke volumes about his growing desire for a shared creative outlet. The sketchbook, a symbol of his past dreams, now represented a collaborative future, a space where they could merge their individual visions.

Sira, touched by his thoughtful gesture, admitted that she'd always secretly admired his artistic talent, a hidden skill overshadowed by his practical, down-to-earth nature. "I always thought my creative side died when I chose accounting," she confessed, a hint of wistfulness in her voice. "But... maybe it didn't." The idea ignited a spark within her, a renewed sense of possibility. They spent the next few weeks brainstorming ideas, sketching out whimsical illustrations, and even incorporating Maya into their creative process, her chubby fingers leaving smudged prints on the pages. The sketchbook, once a solitary pursuit, transformed into a shared diary of their evolving dreams, a tangible representation of their collective aspirations.

Their conversations extended beyond art. They started discussing their long-term goals, weaving together their individual ambitions into a tapestry of shared dreams. Sira, always grounded in practicality, envisioned a stable financial future for their family. She spoke of potentially returning to her accounting career, once Maya was a little older, balancing her professional ambitions with her role as a mother. Keith, equally ambitious, harbored a desire to start his own business, a dream that had been dormant for years. He visualized a small, community-focused venture, possibly a mobile carpentry service, utilizing his skills to build and repair things within their local area.

The initial discussions were hesitant, filled with unspoken anxieties and insecurities. The fear of failure loomed large, amplified by the weight of their responsibilities. But as they talked, they realized that their dreams weren't mutually exclusive; they were complementary, interwoven in a way that strengthened their resolve. Keith's carpentry business could provide a stable income, complementing Sira's accounting expertise. They could pool their resources, sharing the financial burden, and supporting each other through the inevitable challenges. They discussed potential childcare arrangements, acknowledging the need for flexibility and understanding as they navigated the complexities of parenthood and professional life.

The conversations weren't always smooth; disagreements arose, particularly regarding the practicality of Keith's entrepreneurial venture. Sira, ever the pragmatist, voiced her concerns, highlighting the risks and uncertainties involved in starting a business. Keith, while acknowledging her concerns, remained determined to pursue his passion. The key, they discovered, lay not in suppressing their differing perspectives, but in finding a common ground, a shared vision that encompassed both their aspirations.

Their shared dreams went beyond their professional ambitions; they also included aspirations for their family life. They imagined creating a warm, loving home filled with laughter, where Maya could thrive and flourish. They talked about family vacations, adventures that would create lasting memories for their growing family. They envisioned holidays spent with loved ones, creating traditions that would strengthen their family bonds. They imagined reading bedtime stories to their children, sharing their love of books and stories. These seemingly simple aspirations held immense significance, underscoring their commitment to building a strong and loving family unit.

The realization dawned on them that their individual growth and healing were inextricably linked to their shared dreams and goals. Their journey, far from being a solitary path, was a shared odyssey, a testament to their collective strength and resilience. Each milestone, each accomplishment, would be celebrated not just as individual triumphs, but as collective victories, solidifying their bond and deepening their love. The process itself was a testament to their love story; an unfolding chapter defined by mutual respect, unwavering support, and a shared vision for the future.

One evening, nestled on the sofa with Maya asleep between them, Keith brought up the possibility of buying a larger house in a few years. The current house, while cozy, felt increasingly cramped as their family expanded. They discussed the pros and cons, the financial implications, and the emotional attachment they had developed for their current home. Sira, initially hesitant, softened as Keith passionately described his vision: a house with a large garden, a space where Maya could play freely, a home that could accommodate their growing family and their shared dreams.

The conversation flowed organically, devoid of the tension and insecurities that had plagued their relationship in the past. They spoke openly and honestly about their fears and aspirations, their voices laced with a newfound confidence and mutual respect. The realization dawned upon them that their individual growth and healing were inextricably linked to their shared dreams and goals. The shared dreams were not just about material possessions or professional success, but about creating a secure and loving environment for their family, a space where their individual strengths could complement and support each other.

As they talked, a sense of profound peace settled over them. They weren't just navigating the complexities of adult life and parenthood; they were actively creating a future together, a future shaped by their collective hopes and aspirations. Their love, initially tested and challenged, had blossomed into something deeper, stronger, and more resilient. It was a love grounded in shared experiences, mutual respect, and a commitment to building a life together, one dream, one goal, one shared moment at a time.

Their journey had been far from smooth sailing. The financial struggles, the anxieties surrounding Sira's pregnancy, Keith's initial lack of understanding, and the unexpected arrival of Sira's ex-boyfriend had all tested the strength of their bond. But they had emerged from those trials, transformed, stronger, and with a clearer understanding of themselves and each other. Their love story wasn't a fairy tale; it was a realistic portrayal of a relationship navigating the complexities of adult life, shaped by the triumphs and struggles of parenthood, and ultimately strengthened by their shared commitment to love, understanding, and unwavering support.

The future remained uncertain, a canvas awaiting their brushstrokes. But they faced it together, hand-in-hand, their love serving as a compass, guiding them toward a future filled with promise and hope. Their shared dreams and goals were not merely aspirations, but a roadmap, a testament to their resilience, a powerful narrative of growth, healing, and the enduring magic of finding your person amidst the chaos of life. Their love story was a continuous evolution, a dance between challenges and triumphs, a story forever unfolding, a testament to the enduring power of love, a love that had the strength to weather any storm. It was a story about two people, learning, growing, and falling deeper in love with each other, one day at a time. And that, in itself, was the most beautiful dream of all.

Celebrating Milestones

Maya's first giggle echoed through the small, but cozy, house, a sound that instantly erased the lingering anxieties that still occasionally haunted Sira. It was a small victory, a fleeting moment, but it held immense weight. Keith, sprawled on the floor, surrounded by a chaotic landscape of brightly colored toys, looked up, his eyes crinkling at the corners as he grinned. He scooped her up, burying his face in her soft, downy hair. "Did you hear that, sweetheart?" he whispered, his voice thick with emotion. "Our little girl laughed."

Sira, watching them, felt a warmth spread through her chest, a profound sense of contentment she hadn't anticipated. The house, once a symbol of their financial struggles and Keith's impulsive decision, now felt like a sanctuary, a testament to their shared commitment. The walls, painted a soft, calming blue, were adorned with Maya's artwork – a chaotic collection of scribbles and finger paints that somehow managed to capture the vibrancy of their lives. The kitchen, though small, was always filled with the aroma of baking bread or simmering soup, a constant reminder of the warmth and nourishment they shared.

The initial anxieties about Keith's ex-girlfriends had lessened, though not entirely vanished. They still maintained a cordial relationship, attending occasional gatherings with Keith, but the edge of Sira's jealousy had dulled. She had learned to trust Keith, to trust the depth of his love for her and Maya. It hadn't been easy; therapy had been invaluable in helping her navigate her insecurities and understand the source of her anxieties. She realized that her fear wasn't just about Keith's past relationships; it was rooted in her own past experiences, her own insecurities about her worthiness of love and happiness.

The arrival of Maya had profoundly shifted their perspectives. Suddenly, the petty squabbles and disagreements that had once consumed their energy seemed insignificant, inconsequential. Their focus had changed, sharpened; their love had deepened. They were a team, a family unit working together to nurture and protect their daughter.

One Saturday afternoon, Keith surprised Sira with a picnic in the park. Maya, now toddling with unsteady steps, explored the grass, her tiny fingers reaching out to touch the colorful wildflowers. Keith spread out a checkered blanket, laying out a feast of sandwiches, fruits, and Maya's favorite – mashed sweet potatoes. As they ate, surrounded by the laughter of children and the gentle rustling of leaves, Sira felt an overwhelming sense of peace. This was it – the simple, unadulterated happiness she had longed for.

Later that evening, as Maya slept soundly in her crib, Keith held Sira close. "Remember all the worries we had?" he asked softly, his thumb caressing her cheek.

Sira nodded, remembering the sleepless nights, the financial anxieties, the doubts that had threatened to tear them apart. "It seems like a lifetime ago," she whispered.

"We've come so far," Keith said, his voice filled with pride and love. "We've learned, we've grown, and we've built something incredible." He paused, his eyes sparkling with emotion. "We have a family."

That night, they didn't just make love; they celebrated their resilience, their shared triumphs, and the unwavering strength of their love. It was a silent acknowledgment of their journey, a celebration of their ability to overcome adversity and build a strong, loving foundation for their family.

The following weeks were a flurry of milestones. Maya's first steps, her first word ,"dada" much to Sira's playful amusement, her first attempts at crawling – each a small victory that filled their hearts with joy. They documented every moment, capturing the precious memories in photographs and videos. Sira started a scrapbook, meticulously preserving Maya's artwork, tiny handprints, and locks of hair – tangible reminders of their daughter's growth and their own evolving journey as parents.

Keith, surprisingly, took to fatherhood with an unexpected tenderness. He was no longer the impulsive, slightly reckless young man Sira had fallen in love with in college. Fatherhood had softened him, deepened his empathy, and broadened his perspective. He was patient, loving, and fiercely protective of his family. He learned to balance his work life with his responsibilities as a father, always finding time to play with Maya, to read her bedtime stories, and to soothe her when she cried. He even started baking cookies with Maya, creating a messy but joyful tradition in their small kitchen.

Sira, too, had transformed. The insecurities that had plagued her had gradually faded, replaced by newfound confidence and self-assurance. She had discovered a strength within herself that she never knew existed. Motherhood had empowered her, giving her a sense of purpose and fulfillment that went beyond her personal anxieties. She learned to prioritize self-care, understanding that she couldn't pour from an empty cup. She discovered the importance of setting boundaries, of advocating for her needs and her family's needs. She learned to trust her instincts and to rely on her own judgment.

One evening, as they sat on the porch, watching the sunset paint the sky with vibrant hues, Keith put his arm around Sira, pulling her close. "I never thought I'd be this happy," he confessed, his voice husky with emotion.

Sira leaned her head against his shoulder, a wave of emotion washing over her. "Me neither," she whispered. "But we made it work, didn't we?"

"We did," Keith replied, his voice firm and confident. "And we'll keep making it work, no matter what."

Their journey had been far from easy. There had been moments of doubt, of fear, of uncertainty. But through it all, their love had remained their anchor, their guiding light. They had learned to communicate, to compromise, and to forgive. They had faced their challenges head-on, growing stronger and more resilient with each obstacle they overcame.

The unexpected arrival of Sira's high school ex-boyfriend, while initially unsettling, had ultimately strengthened their bond. The encounter had served as a reminder of how far they had come, of how much they had grown as individuals and as a couple. It had been a test, and they had passed with flying colors. They were a team, their love story an ongoing narrative of growth, healing, and the enduring power of commitment. And as they sat there, hand-in-hand, watching the stars emerge in the darkening sky, they knew that their future, though still uncertain, was filled with promise, hope, and an unwavering love that would continue to guide them through whatever life threw their way. Their small victories, their shared milestones, were more than just individual achievements; they were testaments to the resilience of their love, their family, and their shared dream of building a life together. They had found their happy ever after, not in a fairytale ending, but in the quiet moments, the shared laughter, and the unwavering love that bound them together, a love that had grown stronger with each passing day, each challenge overcome, each milestone celebrated. Their love story was far from over; it was just beginning to unfold its most beautiful chapters. And that, in itself, was the most beautiful dream of all.

Chapter 10:

Reflecting on the Journey

The scent of chamomile tea hung in the air, a comforting aroma that did little to soothe the churning in Sira's stomach. Across from her, Keith sat, his usual easy grin replaced with a thoughtful expression. The fire crackled merrily in the hearth of their new home – a home that, just a few months ago, had felt like a distant, impossible dream. Now, it was filled with the soft cries of their newborn daughter, a constant reminder of the whirlwind journey they'd undertaken.

"Remember that first ultrasound?" Keith asked, his voice soft, a ghost of a smile playing on his lips. "I was so nervous, I nearly passed out."

Sira chuckled, the sound a little shaky. "And I was convinced it was all some elaborate prank. A cruel joke from the universe." She traced the delicate curve of her teacup, remembering the sheer terror that had gripped her. The uncertainty, the financial anxieties, the overwhelming fear of the unknown had nearly consumed her. She'd been a mess, a volatile cocktail of hormones and anxieties, lashing out at Keith, at her friends, at the world in general. She'd felt like she was drowning, gasping for air in a sea of uncertainty.

"We were…a mess," Keith admitted, his gaze meeting hers. "I didn't understand. I thought you were trying to push me away, to sabotage things. I was so insecure, so afraid of losing you, that I reacted terribly." He reached across the small space between them, taking her hand in his. His touch was warm, reassuring, a grounding force in the swirling chaos of their memories.

Sira squeezed his hand, the simple gesture conveying a world of unspoken understanding. She thought back to those early therapy sessions, pouring her heart out to Dr. Anya Sharma, confessing her fears, her insecurities, her crippling self-doubt. It had been terrifyingly vulnerable, laying bare her deepest anxieties to a complete stranger, but the process had been transformative. Dr. Sharma had helped her understand the roots of her anxieties, her tendency to self-sabotage, her deep-seated fear of abandonment.

"The therapy was a game-changer," Sira said quietly. "It helped me understand myself, my reactions, my anxieties. I realized I wasn't just being difficult; I was genuinely terrified."

Keith nodded, his eyes filled with empathy. "And I was being a complete idiot. I should have been more supportive, more understanding. I let my own insecurities cloud my judgment. The exes? They were just friends. I should have made that clear from the start."

The memory of those exes, their easy camaraderie with Keith, still stung a little. It had been a constant source of friction, a subtle undercurrent of insecurity that had poisoned their relationship. It was a lesson learned – the importance of clear communication, of honest transparency, of truly seeing your partner's perspective, even when it's uncomfortable.

"We fought, we argued, we nearly broke up countless times," Sira said, a wry smile touching her lips. "It felt like a constant battle, a relentless uphill struggle. But…looking back, those fights were also a form of communication, weren't they? A messy, painful, sometimes ugly form, but communication nonetheless."

Keith chuckled. "Messy is an understatement. Remember that argument about the paint color for the nursery? I still can't believe we nearly ended it over beige versus ivory."

The laughter eased the tension, a gentle wave washing over them, carrying away the weight of their past struggles. They talked for hours, reminiscing about their journey, sharing their vulnerabilities, acknowledging their mistakes, and celebrating their triumphs. They spoke of the financial struggles that had pushed them to the brink, the sleepless nights fueled by caffeine and anxiety, the overwhelming responsibility of becoming parents. They spoke of the fear, the doubt, the sheer exhaustion that had threatened to consume them.

But they also spoke of the moments of pure joy, the shared laughter, the quiet intimacy, the overwhelming love that had bound them together. They talked about the way Keith's hand would instinctively find hers in moments of stress, the way Sira's touch would calm his racing heart. They reminisced about the tiny kicks felt during the pregnancy, the overwhelming rush of emotion during the birth, the first time they looked into their daughter's eyes.

"We learned a lot," Keith said, his voice thick with emotion. "About ourselves, about each other, about what it truly means to be committed, to love unconditionally, to face life's challenges together."

Sira nodded, her heart swelling with gratitude and love. The journey hadn't been easy, far from it. It had been a relentless rollercoaster of emotions, a chaotic blend of joy and pain, of laughter and tears. But it had forged them into something stronger, something more resilient, something more deeply connected.

They had faced financial instability, navigated the treacherous waters of jealousy and insecurity, endured the emotional turmoil of pregnancy and the challenges of new parenthood. They had battled miscommunication, overcome mistrust, and ultimately found a way to communicate effectively, truly hearing each other's concerns and anxieties.

Their relationship wasn't perfect, and it would never be. There would be more challenges, more struggles, more moments of doubt and frustration. But they had built a foundation of trust, of understanding, of unwavering commitment, a foundation that they knew could weather any storm. The challenges they had faced hadn't broken them; they had made them stronger, wiser, and infinitely more in love.

The fire crackled, casting dancing shadows on the walls. Their daughter stirred in her crib, a soft gurgle escaping her lips. Sira looked at Keith, her gaze filled with love, gratitude, and a deep sense of peace. They had come so far, overcome so much. And as they looked ahead, into the uncertain future, they did so together, hand in hand, with a newfound confidence and a shared vision for their future. The journey had been tumultuous, but it had been their journey, and they wouldn't trade it for the world. It was a testament to their love, their resilience, their ability to navigate the complexities of life together, and to emerge stronger on the other side.

The next chapter of their story was unwritten, a blank page awaiting their creation. But they faced it with hope, with optimism, with a deeper understanding of each other and themselves, and with the unshakeable belief that, together, they could conquer anything. The future held both challenges and opportunities – new jobs, new friends, more sleepless nights, the joys of watching their daughter grow. But through it all, they would have each other, their love a guiding light, a beacon of hope in the sometimes turbulent seas of life. They had learned to communicate, to forgive, to understand, and to appreciate the messy, beautiful, unpredictable journey of love and life. And as they held hands, gazing into the dancing flames, they knew this was just the beginning of their happily ever after, a story unfolding one day, one challenge, one tender moment at a time. Their love, tested and refined through adversity, shone brighter than ever before, a testament to the enduring power of commitment, forgiveness, and the unwavering belief in the strength of their bond. The future was uncertain, but they were ready, together, to face whatever came their way.

Embracing the Future

The first few months after Maya's arrival were a blur of sleepless nights, overflowing diapers, and a love so profound it felt like it could shatter the very fabric of their reality. Keith, surprisingly, took to fatherhood with an almost unnerving ease. He'd traded his late-night poker games for bedtime stories, his boisterous laughter for gentle coos as he rocked Maya to sleep. Sira, initially overwhelmed by the sheer responsibility, found herself relying on Keith in ways she hadn't anticipated. The initial anxieties she'd felt about motherhood, about her ability to be a good mother, slowly dissipated as she watched Keith's unwavering support and the pure, unconditional love in his eyes.

Their relationship, once a tumultuous sea of insecurities and misunderstandings, had calmed into a gentler current. The therapy sessions had been invaluable, helping Sira unpack her anxieties and Keith to understand the depths of her emotional landscape. He learned to listen not just to her words, but to the unspoken worries etched on her face, the subtle tremor in her voice. He started anticipating her needs, bringing her a cup of tea before she even realized she was thirsty, offering a comforting hand when the exhaustion threatened to overwhelm her.

The presence of his ex-girlfriends, once a source of immense stress for Sira, had faded into the background. They remained friendly, their interactions cordial and devoid of the undercurrent of tension that had once plagued Sira. She realized that Keith's friendships were his own, separate from their relationship, and that his affection for her was unique and unwavering. The jealousy she had harbored began to dissipate, replaced by a quiet confidence in their love. The surprise visit from her high school ex, Mark, had been a minor blip, quickly forgotten as their lives revolved around the tiny human who had brought them such unexpected joy. Mark's appearance served as a reminder of a past Sira had left behind, a past that paled in comparison to the vibrant present she was creating with Keith.

Financially, things were still tight. The mortgage on their house was a constant weight, but the shared responsibility, the shared burden, somehow felt less daunting than it had before. They found solace in their shared struggles, their combined efforts a testament to their strength as a couple. Keith, now more focused and determined than ever, secured a promotion at his job, his newfound dedication fueled by his desire to provide for his family. Sira, finding a balance between motherhood and her own aspirations, began freelancing, her creative talents finding an outlet in her writing. The financial challenges remained, but they faced them together, shoulder to shoulder, their combined efforts transforming the struggle into an opportunity for growth and teamwork.

Their new home, once a symbol of their anxieties, had transformed into a haven. It was filled with the sounds of Maya's laughter, the aroma of freshly baked bread, and the comforting silence of shared moments. It was a testament to their resilience, a symbol of their enduring love and commitment. The walls, once bare, were now adorned with family photos, childish drawings, and treasured memories. It was a space they were carefully crafting, brick by brick, moment by moment, a space that mirrored the growth of their relationship, the blossoming of their family.

One evening, as Maya slept soundly in her crib, Sira and Keith sat on the porch swing, watching the stars emerge in the twilight sky. The air was crisp and cool, the silence punctuated only by the gentle chirping of crickets. Sira rested her head on Keith's shoulder, feeling the familiar comfort of his presence.

"I never thought I'd be here," Sira whispered, her voice barely audible above the gentle sounds of the night.

Keith squeezed her hand, his thumb caressing her knuckles. "Me neither," he admitted, a soft smile playing on his lips. "But I wouldn't trade it for anything."

"Remember all the doubts, all the fears?" Sira asked, her gaze fixed on the twinkling stars above.

Keith chuckled. "How could I forget? You were convinced I was trying to sabotage your life with my ex-girlfriends, and I was convinced you were using the pregnancy to control me."

Sira laughed, a light, airy sound. "We were a mess."

"A beautiful, chaotic mess," Keith corrected, pulling her closer. "And we've learned so much from it. We've grown so much."

Sira nodded, her eyes shining with unshed tears. "We've learned to communicate, to trust, to forgive. We've learned the true meaning of teamwork, of partnership."

"And of unconditional love," Keith added, his voice thick with emotion. He kissed her forehead, a tender gesture that spoke volumes. "The kind of love that can withstand anything, that can conquer any obstacle."

Their future wasn't devoid of challenges. They knew that life would continue to throw curveballs, that there would be more sleepless nights, more financial anxieties, more moments of doubt. But they were no longer afraid. They had faced the storm together, emerged stronger, and learned to navigate the choppy waters of life as a team. They had found their footing, their balance, their rhythm.

The love they shared was the anchor that kept them grounded, the compass that guided their path. It was a love that had been tested, tried, and refined, a love that shone brighter than ever before. It was a love that had weathered the storm and emerged, triumphant, into the warm embrace of a future filled with hope, optimism, and the unwavering belief in the strength of their bond. It was that love.

They knew that parenting wouldn't always be easy. There would be tantrums, sleepless nights, and the constant challenge of balancing work and family life. But they were ready to face these challenges together, their love serving as the foundation upon which they would build their family. They envisioned family dinners filled with laughter and conversation, weekend adventures exploring new places, and the quiet moments shared between a husband, a wife, and their cherished daughter. They were committed to building a life filled with love, joy, and stability, a life where Maya would grow up knowing the unwavering support and affection of her parents.

Sira's career aspirations also played a significant role in their future plans. She dreamed of publishing her own novel, a project she had put on hold when she became pregnant. Now, with a renewed sense of purpose and the support of Keith, she was ready to pick up where she left off. They discussed the possibility of her working from home, allowing her to balance her writing career with her responsibilities as a mother. Keith promised to be her biggest cheerleader, her rock, her unwavering support system as she pursued her dream.

Keith's career was also undergoing a transformation. His promotion brought not only increased financial security but also a new sense of responsibility and fulfillment. He was committed to excelling in his work, not just for himself but for his family. He knew that his success would provide a better future for Maya and give Sira the freedom to pursue her writing ambitions. The financial stability they were working toward wasn't just about material possessions; it was about providing Maya with opportunities and ensuring a comfortable life for their growing family.

They knew that the road ahead wouldn't always be smooth. There would be disagreements, compromises, and moments of frustration. But they had learned the importance of open communication, of expressing their needs and feelings honestly and respectfully. They had learned to forgive, to understand, and to appreciate each other's strengths and weaknesses. They were no longer the two individuals who had stumbled into a relationship; they were a team, a family, ready to face the world together.

As the night deepened, the stars continued to twinkle above them, their light a metaphor for the hope that burned brightly in their hearts. They held hands, their fingers intertwined, their love a silent promise, a testament to the strength of their bond, a beacon guiding them towards a future they were ready to embrace. Their journey had been challenging, filled with unexpected twists and turns. But as they gazed into each other's eyes, they saw not only a reflection of their shared past but also a vision of their bright future, a future they would build together, one day, one challenge, one tender moment at a time. It was a future filled with promise, a future that held the promise of happiness, stability and a love that would continue to grow and blossom with each passing year. The future was uncertain, but together, they were ready to face it, hand in hand, their hearts filled with unwavering hope and the unshakeable belief in the power of their love.

New Challenges and Opportunities

The first tentative steps Maya took across the living room floor were a milestone, a tiny victory in their ongoing saga. Keith, filming the event on his phone, chuckled as she wobbled, her tiny hands outstretched for balance, her face a mask of determined concentration. Sira, watching from the armchair, felt a familiar swell of emotion – a mixture of pride, exhaustion, and overwhelming love. It was a moment that encapsulated their lives perfectly: small victories amidst the chaos, constant challenges balanced by moments of pure joy.

The arrival of Maya had shifted their dynamic subtly. Sira, once fiercely independent, found herself relying more on Keith, not just for practical help with the baby, but for emotional support. The financial strain, though eased somewhat by Keith's steady job and the sale of his old car, still loomed large. The mortgage payments were a constant pressure, a quiet reminder of the weight of their responsibilities. Yet, the weight was shared, a silent pact between them, unspoken yet powerfully felt.

Keith, ever the pragmatist, had begun to consider his future career options. The stability of a steady job was no longer enough. He craved something more, a career path that would allow them to thrive, not just survive. He started attending evening classes, studying for a certification that would open doors to higher-paying positions in his field. Sira, though initially worried about the added strain, was secretly proud of his ambition, his drive to provide for their family.

Their relationship, too, was evolving. The initial insecurities stemming from Keith's past relationships had largely subsided, replaced by a deeper understanding and a more mature appreciation for each other. The occasional pang of jealousy still surfaced, a fleeting shadow in the bright sunshine of their love, but they learned to address it, to communicate openly and honestly about their fears and vulnerabilities.

Sira's therapy sessions proved invaluable. She learned coping mechanisms to manage her anxiety, strategies to navigate the rollercoaster of emotions that motherhood inevitably brought. The therapist helped her understand that her feelings were valid, that it was okay to feel overwhelmed, even resentful at times. It wasn't a sign of weakness; it was a sign of her strength, her ability to acknowledge her struggles and seek help.

The unexpected visit from Sira's high school ex-boyfriend, Mark, had initially shaken their world. Mark, now a successful lawyer, had appeared seemingly out of the blue, expressing regret for his past mistakes and a desire to reconnect. Sira, initially confused and conflicted, confided in Keith, who, to her surprise, reacted with unexpected maturity. He listened patiently, offering support without judgment, understanding that her past was part of who she was. He knew, instinctively, that their relationship was strong enough to weather this storm.

The encounter with Mark, though seemingly a threat, had actually strengthened their bond. It forced them to confront unspoken anxieties and insecurities, anxieties that had simmered beneath the surface of their daily lives. They talked, not just about Mark, but about their fears and doubts concerning their future, their commitment to each other, and the ever-present challenges of parenting. These conversations, though sometimes painful, were ultimately cathartic, paving the way for a deeper level of intimacy and understanding.

The future, however, remained uncertain, a vast, uncharted territory. They knew that more challenges lay ahead; financial anxieties, the inevitable strains of raising a child, the complexities of a growing family. But they also knew, with a certainty that warmed their hearts, that they would face those challenges together. Their love, forged in the crucible of adversity, had grown stronger, deeper, more resilient than they had ever imagined.

Keith's dedication to his studies was remarkable. He juggled late nights of studying with early mornings of diaper changes and playtime with Maya. He didn't complain, didn't grumble, instead focusing on the bigger picture: a brighter future for his family. Sira, in turn, took on more responsibility around the house, organizing their lives with an efficiency that surprised even herself. She discovered a strength she hadn't known she possessed, a capacity for resilience and resourcefulness that blossomed under pressure.

They started small, making subtle changes in their lifestyle to cut expenses. They cooked more meals at home, cut down on unnecessary spending, and found creative ways to entertain Maya without breaking the bank. The changes weren't glamorous, but they were effective, a testament to their collective determination to build a secure future.

The support system they'd built around themselves also played a significant role in their success. Sira's mother, though initially hesitant about their relationship, had become a steadfast source of support, helping with childcare and offering practical advice on everything from budgeting to baby care. Keith's friends, despite the initial tension caused by Sira's insecurities, had come to accept and appreciate her, realizing the depth of their love and commitment. The once-strained relationships had mellowed, replaced by a newfound respect and understanding.

Their evenings were filled with a quiet intimacy, a shared space between the demands of work, parenting, and personal growth. They read to Maya, bathed her, and snuggled her to sleep, their love for her radiating outwards, a warm glow that permeated their lives. They found time for themselves, too, stealing moments of quiet intimacy amidst the chaos, holding hands while watching a movie, sharing a quiet cup of tea, their eyes communicating a thousand unspoken words.

One evening, as Maya slept soundly in her crib, Keith and Sira sat on the porch swing, the summer breeze rustling through the leaves of the trees. They talked about their dreams, their hopes, their fears. They acknowledged the struggles, the sacrifices, the compromises they'd made, but also celebrated the triumphs, the joys, the immense love that bound them together.

They talked about expanding their family, about the possibility of having more children, about the future they envisioned for Maya. They talked about their individual aspirations, about Keith's career goals and Sira's desire to pursue a creative hobby she'd put aside after Maya's birth. They didn't shy away from the potential challenges – the financial implications, the time constraints, the emotional toll – but they discussed them with a shared sense of purpose, a determination to face whatever came their way, hand in hand.

Their journey hadn't been easy, far from it. It had been a challenging, sometimes painful, but ultimately rewarding experience. It had tested their strength, their patience, their resilience, their love. And through it all, their bond had only grown stronger, their love deeper, their commitment unwavering. They had learned to adapt, to compromise, to communicate, to support each other through thick and thin.

As they looked towards the future, they did so with a newfound confidence, a shared vision of a life filled with love, laughter, challenges, and triumphs. They knew there would be more ups and downs, more challenges and opportunities, but they faced them not with trepidation but with a quiet strength, a shared belief in their love, and a deep understanding of the beautiful, chaotic journey of life together. The path ahead was uncertain, but together, they were ready, prepared to embrace whatever came, secure in the knowledge that their love would be their compass, guiding them through the storm, illuminating their path towards a future filled with hope, promise, and enduring love. The stars above twinkled, mirroring the hope that burned brightly within their hearts, a silent testament to the enduring power of their love story.

A Stronger Foundation

The arrival of Noah, Sira's high school sweetheart, had been a jarring disruption, a ghost from a past Sira had mostly buried. His sudden appearance, a casual encounter at the coffee shop down the street, had stirred up a whirlwind of emotions, both in Sira and in Keith. Noah, charming as ever, had seemed genuinely happy for them, offering congratulations on the baby and expressing admiration for the beautiful life Sira had built with Keith. But the encounter left a lingering unease, a subtle crack in the newly cemented foundation of their relationship.

The following days were a blur of introspection for Sira. She found herself analyzing her feelings, dissecting every word Noah had spoken, every nuance of his expression.

Had she been subtly comparing her current life with Keith to her past with Noah? Was there a flicker of regret? The thought was unsettling, threatening to unravel the carefully constructed peace she had painstakingly built. She knew, deep down, that she loved Keith, that Noah was merely a fleeting memory, a reminder of a younger, less certain self. Yet, the lingering questions, the subtle doubts, were persistent thorns in her side.

Keith, ever observant, noticed the shift in Sira's demeanor. He saw the haunted look in her eyes, the subtle hesitation in her touch. He knew something was bothering her, and he was determined to understand. He didn't accuse her, didn't press for answers, but instead offered quiet support, a comforting presence in the midst of her internal turmoil. He made her a cup of tea, helped her tidy up the living room, and listened patiently as she finally confided in him about her encounter with Noah.

"It wasn't like that," she explained, her voice trembling slightly, "It was just… a reminder. Of who I was, before everything."

Keith took her hand, his touch firm yet gentle. "And who are you now, Sira?" he asked softly.

Sira looked at him, her eyes filled with a newfound clarity. "I'm stronger," she said, her voice filled with conviction, "I'm more confident, more sure of myself. Noah was a part of my past, but Keith… you are my present and my future."

Their conversation stretched late into the night, a deep and honest exchange of vulnerabilities and reassurances. They talked about their fears, their anxieties, their hopes for the future. They discussed the challenges they had faced, the obstacles they had overcome, and the unwavering strength of their love. It was a conversation that solidified their bond, a testament to the depth of their connection.

The following weeks were filled with a quiet intensity. The looming arrival of their baby brought with it a renewed sense of purpose, a shared focus that cemented their commitment. They spent countless hours preparing for the new addition to their family, painting the nursery, assembling furniture, and meticulously planning every detail. The house, once a source of contention, now felt like a sanctuary, a haven filled with love and anticipation. Keith's initial reservations about the house, about the financial strain it placed on them, had completely dissipated. The sheer joy of anticipation for their child had overshadowed any previous anxieties. The house, a symbol of their shared future, represented a culmination of their collective efforts, a testament to their burgeoning strength as a couple.

Sira continued her therapy sessions, finding solace and guidance in her weekly conversations with her therapist. The sessions provided a safe space for her to process her emotions, to navigate the complexities of pregnancy, and to manage the anxieties that occasionally overwhelmed her. She learned to identify her triggers, to recognize her own patterns of insecurity, and to develop healthy coping mechanisms. The therapy helped her understand her own emotional landscape, enabling her to communicate more effectively with Keith and to build a stronger, more resilient relationship.

Keith, in turn, made a conscious effort to understand Sira's anxieties. He acknowledged her fears, validated her emotions, and actively participated in building a more secure and stable environment for their growing family. He recognized the need to reassess his relationships with his ex-girlfriends, understanding that maintaining close friendships could be misinterpreted as a threat by Sira. He didn't cut them off entirely, but he established clearer boundaries, prioritizing his relationship with Sira and ensuring that his interactions with his exes didn't compromise their stability.

The pregnancy progressed smoothly, marked by moments of joy, anticipation, and the occasional bout of morning sickness. Keith was an involved partner, attending every doctor's appointment, helping Sira with chores around the house, and showering her with unwavering affection. He even learned to prepare some of her favorite comfort foods, becoming a skilled chef in the process.

As the delivery date drew closer, Sira felt a surge of confidence, a sense of readiness that hadn't been present earlier in her pregnancy. The initial anxieties, the fears of inadequacy, the insecurities that had plagued her were gradually replaced by a quiet strength, a deep understanding of her own capabilities. She was prepared not only for motherhood but also for the challenges that lay ahead in their relationship.

The birth of their baby girl, Maya, was a transformative event, a watershed moment that redefined their lives. The love they felt for their daughter was overwhelming, a powerful force that strengthened their bond beyond measure. The challenges they had faced, the insecurities they had conquered, all seemed insignificant in comparison to the sheer joy of holding their child in their arms. The experience brought them closer than ever before, forging a connection that transcended the everyday anxieties and frustrations of life.

The initial weeks after Maya's birth were filled with the beautiful chaos of newborn life—sleepless nights, feeding schedules, and constant diaper changes. Yet, amidst the exhaustion, there was an overwhelming sense of fulfillment, a profound love that bound them together. Keith was a devoted father, sharing the responsibilities of caring for Maya with Sira. They worked as a team, supporting each other, sharing the burdens and celebrating the small victories.

They had overcome so much together. The financial struggles, the uncertainties, the insecurities, the anxieties – they had faced them head-on, emerging stronger and more unified. Their relationship, once fragile and fraught with tension, had evolved into a solid foundation, capable of weathering any future storms. The love they shared was not just a romantic connection but a deep, unwavering commitment, a partnership built on mutual respect, understanding, and unwavering support. They had built a family, a home, a life together, and that was a victory greater than any they could have imagined. The future still held uncertainties, but they faced it together, hand-in-hand, ready to embrace whatever challenges lay ahead, secure in the knowledge that their love would guide them through, forever strengthening their bond. Their love story, once a tapestry woven with threads of doubt and insecurity, was now a masterpiece, a testament to their enduring strength and the enduring power of love.

The Lasting Impact of Love

The drive home was quiet, a comfortable silence that spoke volumes. The lingering tension from Noah's appearance had dissipated, replaced by a quiet contentment. Keith reached over, his hand finding Sira's, his fingers intertwining with hers. The simple gesture, so familiar yet always comforting, spoke of a depth of connection that transcended words. He squeezed her hand gently, a silent reassurance.

Sira leaned her head against his shoulder, a sigh escaping her lips. The weight of the past few months, the anxieties, the uncertainties – they seemed to melt away in the warmth of his presence. She'd spent so much time worrying, agonizing over every perceived flaw in their relationship, every potential threat to their future. Noah's reappearance had been a stark reminder of those fears, a temporary resurgence of the insecurities that had plagued her for so long. But now, nestled against Keith, those fears seemed insignificant, dwarfed by the immensity of their love.

"He was… nice," Sira said finally, her voice barely a whisper.

Keith chuckled softly. "Nice? Noah? That's about as descriptive as calling the Grand Canyon 'a big hole'." He paused, then added, more seriously, "But I get it. It brought up things, didn't it? Old feelings, old insecurities."

Sira nodded, her eyes welling up slightly. "It made me realize how far we've come. How much stronger we are now. How much I trust you."

Their journey hadn't been easy. It had been a rollercoaster of emotions, a chaotic blend of joy and fear, laughter and tears. The financial strain, the constant pressure of juggling work and school, the unexpected pregnancy – it had all tested them to their limits. The presence of Keith's ex-girlfriends, though initially a source of contention, had ultimately strengthened their bond. It forced them to confront their insecurities, to communicate openly and honestly, to build a level of trust that went beyond mere words.

Their therapist had been instrumental in guiding them through the rough patches. She had helped them understand each other's perspectives, to navigate the complexities of their relationship with greater empathy and understanding. She'd taught them the importance of healthy communication, of expressing their needs and concerns without fear of judgment. She'd helped Sira confront her own anxieties, her deep-seated insecurities, her fear of inadequacy. And she had helped Keith understand the depth of Sira's fears, her anxieties not born from manipulation, but from a place of deep love and insecurity.

"Remember that first fight about the house?" Keith asked, a grin spreading across his face. "You thought I was trying to control you, buy my way into your heart."

Sira laughed, the sound light and carefree. "And you thought I was trying to sabotage your friendships."

"Guilty as charged," Keith admitted. "But look at us now. We're in this together, stronger than ever. We built a home, not just a house."

Their home wasn't just four walls and a roof; it was a sanctuary, a place of warmth and comfort, a testament to their shared journey. It was filled with laughter and whispered secrets, with the comforting aroma of freshly brewed coffee and the sweet scent of baby powder. It was a haven where love flourished, where fears dissipated, and where dreams took flight.

The thought of their growing family filled them with a sense of profound joy. The baby, a symbol of their enduring love, was a constant reminder of their commitment, a tangible representation of their shared future. They had overcome so much, faced so many challenges, and yet their love had only grown stronger, deeper, more resilient. It was a love that had weathered storms, a love that had been tested and refined, a love that had emerged victorious.

Their story was a testament to the power of resilience, the strength of commitment, and the enduring nature of love. It was a story of two young people, navigating the complexities of adult life, facing seemingly insurmountable obstacles, yet emerging stronger, more unified, more in love than ever before. Their love was not merely a romantic ideal, but a tangible force, shaping their lives, guiding their choices, and leading them towards a brighter, more hopeful future.

The pregnancy, initially a source of stress and anxiety, had ultimately brought them even closer. The shared responsibility, the anticipation of parenthood, had forged a bond between them that was unbreakable. They learned to anticipate each other's needs, to support each other's dreams, to navigate the inevitable bumps in the road with patience and understanding. The process of preparing for the baby, of transforming their home into a welcoming haven for their new arrival, had been a shared act of creation, a testament to their growing commitment.

Keith, initially hesitant and somewhat defensive, had eventually embraced the idea of fatherhood with open arms. He had come to appreciate the depth of Sira's anxieties, understanding that her concerns stemmed not from a desire to isolate him, but from a place of profound love and protectiveness. He learned to listen more attentively, to acknowledge her feelings, and to offer the support and understanding that she so desperately needed. He had discovered strength and hardiness within himself, a capacity for love and devotion that he hadn't known he possessed.

Sira, too, had undergone a transformation. She had learned to trust Keith, to relinquish her anxieties, to embrace the joys and challenges of parenthood with a sense of confidence and hope. She had learned the importance of self-care, the necessity of seeking support when needed, and the power of self-compassion. She had grown as a person, as a partner, as a woman. Their journey together had been a transformative experience, shaping them both into stronger, more resilient individuals.

The arrival of their child would undoubtedly bring new challenges, new anxieties, new uncertainties. But they faced the future with a sense of confidence and hope, secure in the knowledge that their love would guide them through, that their commitment would remain steadfast, that their partnership would endure. Their love story, once a complex tapestry woven with threads of doubt and insecurity, had now evolved into a powerful masterpiece, a testament to the enduring strength of their bond, a symbol of the triumph of love over adversity.

They pulled into the driveway of their home, the house that had once been a source of contention, now a symbol of their shared success, a testament to their enduring commitment. As they stepped out of the car, hand in hand, they looked at their home, bathed in the soft glow of the setting sun, a home filled with love, laughter, and the promise of a bright future.

The future held many uncertainties. The challenges of parenthood would be demanding, the complexities of their relationship would continue to evolve. But they faced these unknowns together, their love a beacon, a guiding light in the darkness. They had overcome so much, faced so many obstacles, yet their love remained strong, a testament to their enduring commitment. They knew their journey was far from over, but they were ready for whatever the future held, confident in the knowledge that their love would always be their anchor, their guiding star.

The memory of Noah's unexpected visit faded into the background, becoming a mere footnote in the unfolding narrative of their life together. It had served as a poignant reminder of their journey, a testament to how far they had come, how much they had overcome. It had been a wake-up call, a temporary disruption, but ultimately, it had only served to strengthen their bond. The love they shared was a powerful force, a resilient entity that had weathered storms and emerged triumphant.

The challenges that lay ahead would be numerous, but they faced them with a newfound confidence, a shared sense of purpose, a deep and unwavering commitment to one another. Their relationship had evolved into something profound, something meaningful, something lasting. It was a relationship built on mutual respect, understanding, communication, and above all, unwavering love.

Their story was a testament to the transformative power of love, a testament to the resilience of the human spirit, a testament to the ability of two people to overcome seemingly insurmountable obstacles and emerge stronger, more united, and more in love than ever before. It was a story of hope, a story of perseverance, a story of enduring love. It was a love story for the ages, a love story that would continue to unfold, chapter by chapter, year by year, forever strengthening their bond, forever shaping their lives, forever illuminating their path.

The sun dipped below the horizon, casting long shadows across their lawn. As they stood there, hand in hand, watching the sky erupt in a kaleidoscope of colors, they felt a profound sense of peace, a deep sense of gratitude, a profound sense of love. Their journey had been far from perfect, but it had been theirs, a unique and precious tapestry woven with threads of joy and sorrow, laughter and tears, challenges and triumphs. And as they looked forward to the future, to the next chapter of their lives, they knew that their love would be their compass, guiding them towards a future filled with happiness, fulfillment, and a love that would last a lifetime. The lasting impact of their love would resonate throughout their lives, shaping their future, defining their destiny, and leaving an indelible mark on the world around them. Their love story, a testament to the enduring power of human connection, would continue to evolve, a timeless masterpiece written in the language of the heart.

Acknowledgments

Writing a book is a solitary journey, but it's one I couldn't have completed without the unwavering support of many incredible people. First and foremost, I want to thank my family and friends for their patience, understanding, and endless cups of coffee (or tea, depending on the day). Your belief in me fueled me through the long nights and challenging moments. A special thank you to those I encountered in this journey, whose insights and feedback were invaluable during the editing process. Your keen eye for detail and unwavering encouragement made all the difference. To my readers, your honest opinions and enthusiastic support are deeply appreciated. You helped me shape this story into what it is today. Finally, thank you to all who helped, for your guidance, expertise, and belief in this story. This book would not be the same without your contributions.

Author Biography

I am a novelist learning young adult and new adult fiction. Some of my works explore the complexities of relationships, the challenges of navigating adult life, and the importance of overcoming personal obstacles. I am passionate about crafting authentic and relatable characters that readers can connect with on an emotional level. In my free time, I enjoy a lot of different things, that stem from discovering the world we live in. Willie S' previous works include For the Anur, in the Sci-Fi book category.

www.ingramcontent.com/pod-product-compliance
Lightning Source LLC
LaVergne TN
LVHW011941060526
838201LV00061B/4177